30 minute
entertaining

30 minute
entertaining

Cook modern recipes for entertaining in 30 minutes or less including ingredients such as arugula, shrimp, pumpkin, coconut, swordfish, sesame seeds, rice noodles, champagne, artichokes, prosciutto, and seasonal berries.

Louise Pickford
Photography by Ian Wallace

LAUREL GLEN

First published in North America in 2000 by
Laurel Glen Publishing
An imprint of the Advantage Publishers Group
5880 Oberlin Drive, San Diego, CA 92121-4794
www.advantagebooksonline.com

All notations of errors or omissions should be addressed to Laurel Glen
Publishing, editorial department, at the above address. All other
correspondence (author inquiries, permissions and rights) concerning the
content of this book should be addressed to Hamlyn, an imprint of Octopus
Publishing Group Ltd, 2–4 Heron Quays, London E14 4JP.

ISBN   1-57145-671-6 (hardcover)
         1-57145-677-5 (paperback)

Library of Congress Cataloging-in-Publication Data
Pickford, Louise.
   30 minute entertaining / Louise Pickford ; photography by Ian Wallace.
     p. cm.
   ISBN 1-57145-671-6 -- ISBN 1-57145-677-5 (soft cover)
   1. Quick and easy cookery. 2. Entertaining. I. Title: Thirty minute entertaining. II.
Title.

TX833.5. P53 2000
641.5'55--dc21

                                                    00-044372

Printed in China.

1 2 3 4 5   00 01 02 03 04

Notes

1 Standard level spoon measurements are used in all recipes.

2 Eggs should be medium unless otherwise stated. The USDA advises that
   eggs should not be consumed raw. This book contains dishes made with
   raw or lightly cooked eggs. It is prudent for more vulnerable people, such
   as pregnant and nursing mothers, invalids, the elderly, babies, and young
   children, to avoid uncooked or lightly cooked dishes made with eggs. Once
   prepared, these dishes should be kept refrigerated and used promptly.

3 Milk should be whole unless otherwise stated.

4 Fresh herbs should be used unless otherwise stated. If unavailable, use
   dried herbs as an alternative, but halve the quantities stated.

5 Pepper should be freshly ground black pepper unless otherwise
   stated.

6 Ovens should be preheated to the specified temperature—if using a
   convection oven, follow the manufacturer's instructions for adjusting the
   time and the temperature.

7 This book includes dishes made with nuts and nut derivatives. It is
   advisable for customers with known allergic reactions to nuts and nut
   derivatives and those who may be potentially vulnerable to these allergies,
   such as pregnant and nursing mothers, invalids, the elderly, babies, and
   children, to avoid dishes made with nuts and nut oils. It is also prudent to
   check the labels of prepared ingredients for the possible inclusion of
   nut derivatives.

8 Vegetarians should look for special labeling on cheese to ensure that it is
   made with vegetarian rennet. There are vegetarian forms of Parmesan, feta,
   cheddar, Cheshire, Red Leicester, dolcelatte, and many goat cheeses, among
   others.

Executive Editor: Polly Manguel
Project Editor: Sharyn Conlan
Copy-editor: Linda Doeser
Creative Director: Keith Martin
Senior Designer: David Godfrey
Production Controller: Lisa Moore
Photographer: Ian Wallace
Stylist: Clare Hunt
Home Economist: Louise Pickford

North American Edition
Publisher: Allen Orso
Managing Editor: JoAnn Padgett
Project Editor: Elizabeth McNulty

contents

introduction

I think I probably fell in love with food years before I became aware of just how much I really do love it. Growing up on a farm where good-quality meat, dairy products, vegetables, and fruit were taken for granted, I assumed all food tasted that way. Boarding school food soon changed all that, but as a typical teenager there were other priorities and the enjoyment of food came down to what was in the convenience store.

I can't pretend to have shown much interest in cooking at home. My mother was and still is a great cook, but with no disrespect, her food was unadventurous. It was simply great traditional British cooking. I suspect I did very little to help, but I must have inherited my mother's love of food because I have become an enthusiastic and passionate cook.

Today I make my living by cooking and writing recipes and I feel just as passionate now as I did when I began about 14 years ago. What has changed are the sources of my inspirations through travel, the availability of fresh produce, and people's lifestyles, and attitudes toward cooking. All of these factors have gone into defining the recipes in this book.

With increased awareness of the different cultures around the world, the result of exposure to travel and the media, new and exciting products, and foods with a more exotic nature have become almost commonplace. Supermarkets stock ingredients that until recently were enjoyed only in their native countries. Many of these travel well and can be used to great effect, particularly staples, canned, and bottled foods. However, some imported fresh ingredients have been picked underripe and never produce the flavor they would have had if left to ripen on the plant.

I cook professionally every day, so when I do cook for pleasure for myself, family, or friends I don't want to spend hours preparing ingredients. Similarly, with most people's lifestyles, leisure time is at a premium. Quick, simple, and delicious food is of the highest importance, and I hope that the dishes in this book satisfy those criteria. I have thought hard about the way we eat and the occasions when we may be entertaining, so that you should be able to find a recipe for every event, time of year, and time of day. For instance, this book begins with the first meal of the day—breakfast—but also includes brunch dishes and recipes for mid-morning snacks. The collection of party foods is very useful as it proves that canapés don't have to be excruciatingly intricate and time-consuming to impress. Dinner parties for two or more don't need to take hours to put together or cause any stress, as you'll find plenty of recipes in the Two's Company and Posh Nosh chapters that can be prepared with ease.

PRACTICALITIES

All the recipes in the book have been developed so that they can be prepared and cooked within 30 minutes. It has been quite a challenge to achieve this, as you do not want to compromise the flavor of the dish just to make it quickly. (There are other occasions when you can putter and time is of no consequence.) So I have selected dishes that meet both criteria—to taste great but take no more than 30 minutes.

Of course there are many dishes that are ready in a flash, especially those with little or no cooking involved. You will find that about 40 of the recipes can be ready in under 20 minutes, which really is "fast" food.

The 30 minutes stated includes all the preparation on the assumption that the oven has been preheated, water for cooking pasta is already boiling, and so on. This is so that I can offer a wide range of recipes and it seems mad to omit a recipe because you have to wait an extra 10 minutes for the oven to come to the required temperature. The recipes are easy to follow and very organized—you can be chopping vegetables while the pasta is cooking, for example. Read the recipes through before you start, get pots and pans ready, heat the serving plates, and dishes, and the rest is a breeze.

Nearly all the ingredients in the book are widely available and the glossary will clarify queries on any of the unusual products and where they can be found. It is important in all cooking to buy the freshest produce available, so always shop at a reliable store that you know well, especially for fresh fish and meat. Vegetables and fruit can be found in supermarkets, but a good-quality greengrocer will offer even fresher ingredients, and it's always worth a trip to ethnic food stores, not only for the freshest of ingredients, but simply to view the range of unusual and fascinating foods—most large cities will have at least one Asian food store.

Herbs used are always fresh unless otherwise stated; you can keep fresh herbs wrapped in a plastic bag in the refrigerator for 3–4 days. I recommend sea salt and always crush peppercorns just before using to get the maximum flavor. Olive oil, for use on salads, should be extra virgin, preferably from a single estate, which will be indicated on the bottle. Meat should be free-range where possible, not just for the ethics, but because it really will have more flavor than intensively reared meats.

Sharing food with friends should be a relaxing and sociable pastime. It doesn't have to be a formal event or a meal on a grand scale—a simple supper or lunch with a glass or two of wine, *al fresco* in the summer, is time out from an otherwise hectic day. All this in under 30 minutes—a culinary nirvana!

glossary

Black sesame seeds
These are the same as the more familiar pale golden sesame seeds used extensively in Middle Eastern and Asian cooking. Use in the same way, roasting before use to add a delicious nutty flavor to foods.

Buttermilk
Originally the name given to the liquid extracted from cream during the butter making process. Today "cultured butter-milk" is made with skimmed milk and treated with a fermentation culture and then heat-treated to kill bacteria. It has a very slight sourness and is mainly used in baking—it is especially good for scones.

Chili sauce
Many varieties are available in super-markets, but I recommend a trip to an Asian store to buy an authentic brand.

Cocktail tartlet cases
Ready-made tartlet cases are available in specialist food stores and some larger supermarkets, and are modern variations of vol-au-vent cases. Simply add a filling and serve.

Cordials and syrups
There are a wide variety of fruit, flower and berry cordials available today and they all make a valuable addition to our pantrys. Use not only as a base for

drinks, but add to sweet and savory dishes as an alternative to honey.

Crab meat
White crab meat is available fresh in vacuum packs from good fishmongers, or you can buy mixed crab meat either frozen or prepared in the shell.

Fish sauce
Essential in the cooking of Southeast Asia, fish sauce is made by fermenting small fish in brine. The liquid that is drawn off is then matured in the sun before being bottled. Use in a similar way to soy sauce for adding flavor to foods. It is called *nam pla* in Thailand or *nuoc mam* in Vietnam.

Five-spice seasoning
This is a mixture of ground spices used in Chinese cooking. It is a combination of star anise, cloves, fennel, cassia (Chinese cinnamon), and Szechuan pepper. Add sparingly to savory dishes as the flavor is intense.

Framboise
A raspberry liqueur similar to cassis, used as a mixer for wine and Champagne cocktails.

Horseradish
Fresh horseradish, in season during spring, is rarely available in our stores, although it can be ordered from some greengrocers. Use grated horseradish, available in jars from larger supermarkets, food specialists, or Jewish food stores.

Jerk seasoning
A ready-made spice mix used in West Indian and Creole cooking. It is made up from allspice, cinnamon, nutmeg, thyme, sugar, and chili.

Jerusalem artichokes
These tubers originating from North America, are not related to globe

artichokes. They are knobby greyish brown tubers, roughly oval in shape. They have a sweet, nutty flavor and can be roasted or boiled and mashed.

Kecap manis
This is the name given to sweet soy sauce in Indonesia. It is available in bottles from most supermarkets and Asian stores.

Lemongrass
This is a grass indigenous to tropical Asia, with a pungent lemon flavor that is released when the stalk is crushed or cut. It is used extensively in Asian cooking to flavor soups and stews and is now widely available in super-markets.

Lime leaves
These come from a lime commonly called "kaffir" lime. However, this is not its true name, which is makrut lime. The leaves have an intense aromatic lime flavor which is released when the leaves are torn or bruised. Use to flavor many dishes in Thai, Vietnamese, and Malay cooking.

Marinated artichokes
Small artichokes that have been cooked, charred, and then stored in oil. Available from Italian delicatessens and specialty food stores.

Mirin
Not rice wine, as it is often mistakenly called, but a spirit-based drink used in Japanese cooking. It has a high alcohol content and is added to marinades, sauces, and soups. You can use sake instead, but remember that mirin is sweeter, so add a little sugar.

Miso
A Japanese fermented "bean paste" available from Japanese stores and health food shops. It is available as rice, barley, or rye miso and you can use any one as preferred.

Mussels
Farmed mussels are becoming more readily available and are ideal for the recipes in this book, as they tend to be far cleaner than those that live and grow in the "wild." Consequently, they are quicker and easier to clean.

Nori
These are the flat sheets of seaweed used to make sushi. Available from some supermarkets and health food stores.

Olive paste
Made from black olives and sold in jars.

Palm sugar
This unprocessed sugar is obtained from various palms or from sugarcane and is commonly used as a sweetener in Southeast Asia. It is sold in cylindrical shapes, rounded cakes, or in jars and the color varies from pale gold to dark brown. It is sometimes called jaggery.

Pea shoots
The shoots from young peas, these are generally available only to those who are lucky enough to grow their own. However, some herb and salad suppliers are beginning to sell pea shoots, so keep an eye open as supermarkets are bound to follow.

Pomegranate syrup
This thick, dark syrup, extracted from sour pomegranates, is widely used in North African and Middle Eastern cooking. It has a sharp-sweet flavor. Available from specialist food stores, it has no real equivalent.

Quince paste
Made from the quince fruit, which is a member of the apple and pear family, quince paste or preserve can be traced back to classical times. It is sometimes sold as membrillo paste (the Spanish name) and can be found in some supermarkets or specialty food stores.

Rice flour pancakes
Sold dried, these are very thin rice round flour pancakes that need to be re-hydrated before use. Follow the package instructions.

Rice noodles
Noodles made from rice flour, used in Asian cooking. There are two main types that are sold dried: rice vermicelli noodles, which are thin threads, and the larger flat rice noodles, which are similar to tagliatelle.

Rosewater
First used by the ancient Greeks, Egyptians and Romans, this fragrant water was extracted from roses and added to sweet and savory dishes. Available from Middle Eastern stores and some supermarkets.

Sake
A strong alcoholic Japanese drink often referred to as rice wine, it is used extensively in Japanese cooking. Mirin can be used instead.

Soba noodles
These are Japanese buckwheat noodles, sold dried and widely available from health food stores.

Thai seven-spice seasoning
A ready mix of Thai spices.

Smoke mix
Smoking foods over a mixture of tea leaves, sugar, and rice is common in Chinese cooking and adds an intensely smoky flavor to fish and meat. For the recipes in this book, mix 8 tablespoons each of Jasmine tea leaves, soft brown sugar, and long-grain rice.

Tamarind pulp
Extracted from the pod of the tamarind tree which is a native of Africa, India, and the Far East. The seeds are surrounded by this thick gooey pulp which has a pleasantly sour taste. It is often used to flavor soups, stews, and pastes in Southeast Asian dishes. Available ready-pulped from some supermarkets and Asian food shops.

morning foods

Many of us have such hectic lifestyles that breakfast has become nothing more than a quick cup of coffee and, perhaps, toast or a bowl of cereal. We all know that eating a good breakfast is vital in kick-starting both body and mind into action. The following recipes are designed to do just that, so whether it's a weekday breakfast, weekend brunch, or just a mid-morning snack, take a few extra moments and treat yourself.

Preparation time 5 minutes Cooking time 5 minutes Total time 10 minutes Serves 4

boiled egg
with anchovy soldiers

8 anchovy fillets in oil, drained
2 tbsp. unsalted butter, softened
4 large eggs
4 thick slices white bread
pepper
mustard and watercress, to serve

Boiled eggs with fingers of toast, or "soldiers," is a reminder of childhood. Who wants to grow up, anyway?

one Wash the anchovies, pat dry with paper towels, and then chop finely. Beat them into the butter and season with pepper.

two Boil the eggs for 4–5 minutes, until softly set. Meanwhile, toast the bread, butter one side with the anchovy butter, and cut into fingers.

three Serve the eggs with the anchovy toasts and some mustard and watercress.

Preparation time 5 minutes Cooking time 10–12 minutes Total time 15–17 minutes Serves 4

poached eggs with prosciutto
and herb tomatoes

4 ripe tomatoes
2 tbsp. chopped basil
4 tbsp. extra virgin olive oil
4 slices prosciutto
4 large eggs
salt and pepper
hot buttered English muffins, to serve

This is a healthier version of a traditional "fry-up."

one Halve the tomatoes and place, cut-side up, on a broiler pan. Mix the basil with 2 tbsp. of the oil and drizzle over the cut tomatoes. Season well with salt and pepper. Cook under a preheated broiler for about 6–7 minutes, until softened. Remove and keep warm.

two Meanwhile, heat the remaining oil in a frying pan and fry the prosciutto until crisp. Drain on paper towels and keep warm.

three Poach the eggs in gently simmering water or an egg poacher for 3–4 minutes. Serve on buttered, toasted English muffins with the ham and grilled tomatoes.

Preparation time 10 minutes Cooking time 3–4 minutes per batch, 16 minutes for 12

Total time 26 minutes Serves 4–6

buttermilk pancakes with blueberry sauce

8 oz. fresh blueberries
2 tbsp. honey
dash of lemon juice
½ tsp. butter
1¼ cups self-rising flour
1 tsp. bicarbonate of soda
3 tbsp. sugar
1 egg, beaten
¾ cup buttermilk
yogurt or crème fraîche, to serve
powdered sugar, for dusting

one Warm the berries with the honey and a dash of lemon juice in a small saucepan for about 3 minutes, or until they release their juices. Keep warm.

two Melt the butter in a small pan. Sift the flour and bicarbonate of soda together into a bowl and stir in the sugar. Beat the egg and buttermilk together and gradually whisk into the dry ingredients with the melted butter to make a smooth batter.

three Heat a nonstick frying pan until hot and drop in large spoonfuls of batter. Cook for 3 minutes, or until bubbles appear on the surface. Flip the pancakes over and cook for another minute. Keep warm while cooking the rest.

four Serve the pancakes topped with the blueberry sauce and some yogurt or crème fraîche. Dust with some powdered sugar to decorate.

Preparation time 10 minutes, plus cooling Cooking time 2 minutes Total time 20 minutes Serves 4

tropical fruits with spiced syrup

1 lime
1 piece of stem ginger, diced
2 tbsp. syrup from the ginger jar
2 star anise
4 tbsp. water
½ large cantaloupe melon
1 large mango
1 large papaya
½ pomegranate, to decorate (optional)
fromage frais, to serve

The perfect breakfast for a summer's morning.

one Peel the lime and cut the rind into thin strips. Squeeze the lime juice into a small pan. Add the stem ginger to the pan with the lime rind, ginger syrup, star anise, and water. Simmer for 2 minutes and immediately plunge the base of the pan into some iced water to cool the syrup.

two Meanwhile, prepare the fruit. Cut the cantaloupe into quarters, remove the seeds and cut the flesh into wedges. Peel the mango, remove the stone, and cut the flesh into quarters. Peel and seed the papaya and quarter the flesh.

three Arrange the fruits on plates, spoon over the syrup, decorate with a few pomegranate seeds, if using, and serve with fromage frais.

Preparation time 5 minutes Cooking time 10 minutes Total time 15 minutes Serves 2

herb omelette with mustard mushrooms

1 tbsp. wholegrain mustard
2 tbsp. butter, softened
4 flat mushrooms
2 tbsp. chopped, mixed herbs
(such as chives, parsley, and tarragon)
4 eggs
salt and pepper

If you prefer, cook half the egg mixture at a time to make two smaller omelettes.

one Beat the mustard into 1½ tbsp. of the butter and spread over the undersides of the mushrooms. Place on an aluminum foil lined broiler pan and cook for 5–6 minutes until golden and tender. Remove and keep warm.

two Meanwhile, beat the herbs into the eggs and season to taste with salt and pepper.

three Melt the remaining butter in an omelette or nonstick frying pan, swirl in the egg mixture, and cook until almost set. Carefully slide and flip over on to a warmed plate, add the mushrooms, and serve.

celeriac rösti with smoked eel and horseradish

8 oz. celeriac, finely grated
8 oz. waxy potatoes, finely grated
4 thyme sprigs
2 tbsp. extra virgin olive oil
6 oz. smoked eel fillets
2 tsp. grated horseradish
4 tbsp. crème fraîche
salt and pepper
lemon wedges, to garnish
peppery salad leaves, to serve (optional)

Add some peppery salad leaves dressed with olive oil and lemon juice if you are serving this as a brunch dish.

one Combine the celeriac and potatoes in a bowl. Strip the thyme stalks of their leaves, add the leaves to the vegetables, and season with plenty of salt and pepper. Shape into four large cakes about 4 in. in diameter and 1 in. deep.

two Heat the oil in a large nonstick frying pan, add the cakes, and fry for 5 minutes on each side, or until browned and reduced in height. Drain on paper towels.

three Meanwhile, carefully flake the eel and toss with the horseradish and crème fraîche. Season to taste with salt and pepper.

four Top each rösti with the smoked eel mixture and serve with lemon wedges and some salad leaves, if desired.

18. morning foods

honeyed ricotta with summer fruits

4 oz. raspberries
2 tsp. rosewater
2 tbsp. pumpkin seeds
8 oz. ricotta cheese
8 oz. mixed summer berries
2 tbsp. honey with honeycomb
pinch of ground cinnamon

one Rub the raspberries through a fine strainer to purée, then mix with the rosewater. Alternatively, process them together in a food processor or blender, and then sieve to remove the seeds. Toast the pumpkin seeds.

two Slice the ricotta into wedges and arrange on plates with the berries. Drizzle over the honey and raspberry purée, adding a little honeycomb, and serve scattered with the pumpkin seeds and cinnamon.

lemon and cinnamon crêpes

½ tbsp. butter
1 cup all-purpose flour
½ tsp. ground cinnamon
a pinch of salt
1 tsp. grated lemon rind
1 egg, beaten
1 cup milk
vegetable oil, for frying

To serve
sugar
lemon wedges

one Melt the butter in a small pan. Sift the flour, cinnamon, salt, and grated lemon rind into a bowl, make a well in the center, and gradually beat in the egg, milk, and melted butter to make a smooth batter.

two Lightly brush a crêpe pan or small frying pan with vegetable oil. Heat until smoking, then pour in a small ladleful of batter, swirling it to the edges of the pan.

three Cook for 1 minute until lightly golden underneath, then gently flip over and cook for another 30 seconds. Keep warm while cooking the remainder.

four Serve 2–3 crêpes per person, dusted with sugar and with some lemon wedges.

20. morning foods

Preparation time 15 minutes Cooking time 12 minutes Total time 27 minutes Makes 9

spiced chocolate pastries

8 oz. puff pastry, thawed if frozen
flour, for dusting
1 egg yolk
2 tbsp. milk
18 squares dark chocolate
1 tsp. grated orange rind
a pinch of ground star anise
butter, for greasing

Delicious with a mug of tea or freshly brewed coffee.

one Roll the pastry out thinly on a clean, lightly floured surface and trim to form a 9 in. square. Cut into three, crosswise and lengthwise, to form 9 squares.

two Beat the egg yolk and milk to make a glaze and brush a little around the edges of the squares.

three Place 2 squares of chocolate, a little orange rind, and a touch of star anise on each one. Fold diagonally in half and press the edges together to seal.

four Place the pastries on a greased baking sheet and bake in a preheated 400°F oven for 12 minutes, until puffed and golden. Cool on a wire rack for a few minutes before serving.

Preparation time 12 minutes Cooking time 12 minutes Total time 24 minutes Serves 6

triple chocolate muffins

2 oz. plain chocolate chips
2 tbsp. unsalted butter
2 eggs
6 tbsp. sugar
¾ cup self-rising flour
1 oz. cocoa powder
1 oz. white chocolate chips

one Melt the plain chocolate chips and butter together in a small pan over low heat. Beat the eggs, sugar, flour, and cocoa powder together in a bowl. Fold in the melted chocolate mixture and the white chocolate chips.

two Spoon into a muffin tin lined with paper liners and bake in a preheated 350°F oven for 12 minutes, or until puffed and firm to the touch.

three Transfer to a wire rack to cool slightly before eating.

Preparation time 10 minutes Cooking time 12 minutes Total time 22 minutes Makes 20

quick hazelnut melts

2 oz. blanched hazelnuts
4 tbsp. butter, softened, plus extra
for greasing
¼ cup sugar
1¼ cups all-purpose flour

Hazelnut cookies that literally "melt" in the mouth.

one Grind the hazelnuts in a food processor until fairly smooth, but still retaining a little texture. Dry-fry in a heavy-bottomed frying pan over a low heat until evenly golden. Tip into a bowl and stir until cool.

two Process the butter and sugar together in a food processor until creamy. Add the flour and cooled nuts and process again to make a soft dough.

three Take walnut-size pieces of dough and shape into rolls, then pat into flat ovals. Place on a greased baking sheet and bake in a preheated 375°F oven for 12 minutes, or until just golden. Cool on a wire rack.

Preparation time 10 minutes Total time 10 minutes Serves 2

melon and ginger cooler

1 large ripe galia melon, halved and seeded
4 mint sprigs
1 in. piece of fresh ginger, peeled and grated
1 tbsp. lime cordial
1 tbsp. lime juice
a handful of crushed ice

one Scoop the melon flesh into a food processor or blender. Strip the mint leaves from the stalks. Add the mint leaves, ginger, lime cordial, and lime juice to the melon and process until smooth.

two Half-fill two tall glasses with crushed ice and top off with the melon purée. Serve immediately.

cardamom coffee affogato

4 tbsp. fresh espresso coffee beans
seeds from 2 cardamom pods
4–8 scoops vanilla ice cream
crystal sugar sticks, to serve
(optional)

This spiced coffee takes its name from the Italian word for drowning—the scoops of ice cream slowly "drown" in the coffee making this a real mid-morning treat. It can also be served as an after-dinner coffee or with chocolate ice cream for a mocha flavor.

one Grind the beans and cardamom seeds together in a spice grinder until they are sufficiently ground for your coffeemaker.

two Make a pot of strong coffee in the normal way using the newly ground cardamom coffee and pour into coffee cups or heat-proof glasses.

three Add the ice cream to the coffee and serve immediately with crystal sugar sticks, if using.

mango and coconut lassi

1 large ripe mango
juice of 1 orange
juice of 1 lime
1 tbsp. honey
1 cup yogurt
4 tbsp. coconut milk
ice cubes, to serve

one Peel the mango, cut out the pit, and finely dice the flesh (you will need about 8 oz). Place the flesh in a food processor or blender.

two Add the orange juice, lime juice, honey, yogurt, and coconut milk and process until smooth. Chill or serve immediately with some ice cubes.

light
lunches

Over the past 30 years or so, the way we work has determined the way we eat and today the main meal is in the evening. A leisurely lunch is a bit of a treat, especially midweek, so why not indulge yourself and friends with one of the following dishes? Light and quick to prepare, you can satisfy your hunger without overdoing it!

Preparation time 20 minutes Cooking time 10 minutes Total time 30 minutes Serves 4

noodle soup
with shrimp tempura

4 oz. soba noodles
12 raw tiger shrimp
1 bunch scallions, trimmed
2 bok choy
2 sheets nori
2 tsp. sesame oil
6 cups hot vegetable stock
4 tbsp. sake
2 tbsp. dark soy sauce
4 oz. bean sprouts
vegetable oil, for deep-frying

Tempura
1 egg yolk
½ cup all-purpose flour
7 tablespoons iced water

one Cook the noodles according to package instructions. Meanwhile, peel and devein the shrimp (see page 33). Heat the vegetable oil to 350–375°F, or until a cube of bread browns in 30 seconds.

two To make the soup, slice the scallions and shred the bok choy and nori.
Heat the sesame oil in a large wok and stir-fry the scallions and bok choy for 1 minute. Add the stock, sake, soy sauce, and sugar and simmer gently for 5 minutes. Then stir in the bean sprouts.

three Meanwhile make the tempura batter. Whisk the egg yolk, flour, and water together briefly to make a slightly lumpy batter. Dip the shrimp in the batter and deep-fry in the hot oil for 3 minutes, or until golden. Drain on paper towels.

four Divide the noodles between serving bowls, add the soup, and top with the shrimp and strips of nori.

chilled gazpacho with indian flavors

1 small red onion, chopped
2 garlic cloves, chopped
1 in. piece of fresh ginger, peeled and grated
1 small red pepper, seeded and chopped
2 fresh red chilies, seeded and chopped
1 lb. ripe tomatoes, chopped
2 tbsp. chopped cilantro
4 poppadums, crumbled
1 cup cold vegetable stock
1 cup tomato juice
4 tbsp. extra virgin olive oil
2 tbsp. white wine vinegar
salt and pepper

To garnish
yogurt
poppadums
cilantro sprigs

A classic gazpacho is given an exotic twist with the addition of Indian spices and poppadums. Very refreshing on a hot summer's day.

one Place the onion, garlic, ginger, red pepper, chilies, tomatoes, cilantro, and poppadums in a food processor or blender and process until smooth.

two Transfer to a bowl and stir in the remaining ingredients. Season to taste with salt and pepper. Freeze for at least 10 minutes or until chilled.

three Spoon into soup bowls and serve garnished with yogurt, poppadums, and cilantro sprigs.

goat cheese soufflés

1 tbsp. unsalted butter
½ oz. Parmesan cheese, grated
1 tbsp. plain flour
5 tbsp. milk
1 tbsp. chopped tarragon
1 egg yolk
3½ oz. goat cheese, diced
3 egg whites
salt and pepper

Delicious light and fluffy cheese soufflés.

one Melt half the butter. Brush the insides of 4 ramekin dishes with half the butter and dust with the Parmesan. Place on a baking sheet.

two Melt the remaining butter and stir in the flour. Cook over low heat, stirring constantly, for 30 seconds. Remove from the heat and gradually stir in the milk. Return to the heat and stir until the mixture boils and thickens. Transfer to a bowl.

three Beat the tarragon into the sauce with the egg yolk and goat cheese. Season lightly with salt and pepper. Whisk the egg whites and fold in.

four Spoon into the ramekins and bake in a preheated 400°F oven for 12 minutes, until puffed and golden. Serve immediately.

Preparation time 10 minutes Cooking time 14 minutes Total time 24 minutes Serves 4

charred leek salad with hazelnuts

1 lb. baby leeks
1–2 tbsp. hazelnut oil
dash of lemon juice
1½ oz. blanched hazelnuts
2 little gem or romaine lettuce hearts
a few mint sprigs
½ oz. pecorino cheese
20 black olives, to garnish

Dressing
4 tbsp. hazelnut oil
2 tbsp. extra virgin olive oil
2 tsp. sherry vinegar
salt and pepper

one Brush the leeks with a little hazelnut oil and grill or broil, turning frequently, for 6–8 minutes, or until evenly browned and cooked through. Toss with a dash of lemon juice and season to taste with salt and pepper. Set aside to cool.

two Meanwhile, dry-fry the nuts until browned, cool slightly, and then coarsely chop. Separate the lettuce leaves and pull the mint leaves from the stalks.

three Arrange the leeks in bowls or on plates and top with the lettuce leaves, mint, and nuts. Whisk the dressing ingredients together and pour over the salad. Shave the pecorino over the salad and serve garnished with the olives.

Preparation time 8 minutes Cooking time 20 minutes Total time 28 minutes Serves 4

spinach, artichoke, and bacon salad with a warm dressing

4 small Jerusalem artichokes
2 tbsp. walnut oil
8 slices smoked pancetta
1½ oz. walnuts
4–6 tbsp. extra virgin olive oil
1 garlic clove, crushed
2 tbsp. balsamic vinegar
4 oz. baby spinach leaves
2 oz. watercress
4 tbsp. chopped mixed herbs (such as basil, chervil, mint, and parsley)
salt and pepper

one Scrub the artichokes well and cut into ¼ in. thick slices. Toss with the walnut oil in a roasting pan or ovenproof dish and roast in a preheated 400°F oven for 20 minutes, turning halfway through the cooking time.

two Meanwhile, grill the pancetta until it is crisp and then break it into bite-sized pieces. Dry-fry the walnuts, stirring constantly, until evenly browned. Set aside.

three Heat 1 tbsp. of the olive oil in a small pan and sauté the garlic for 1 minute, until lightly golden. Add the vinegar and remaining olive oil, season to taste with salt and pepper, and keep warm.

four Place the spinach leaves and watercress in a large bowl and add the pancetta, walnuts, artichokes, and herbs and mix well. Arrange the salad on serving plates and drizzle on the warm dressing. Serve immediately.

sesame steamed shrimp

16 raw tiger shrimp, peeled, with tails intact
and deveined (see right)
2 garlic cloves, sliced
1 red chili, seeded and chopped
grated rind and juice of 1 lime
1 in. piece ginger, peeled and chopped
2 tbsp. rice wine
2 tbsp. Thai fish sauce
4 Savoy cabbage leaves
1 tbsp. sesame oil
salt
a few cilantro, mint, and basil leaves,
to garnish

To devein shrimp, cut down the length of the middle of the curved back of the peeled shrimp with a sharp knife. Remove the intestinal vein with the tip of the knife or your fingers.

one First butterfly the shrimp. Cut down the deveined slit on the back of the prawns so they will open up and lie flat, leaving the tail intact. Wash and pat dry.

two Combine the garlic, chili, lime rind and juice, ginger, rice wine, and fish sauce in a large bowl. Add the shrimp and toss well to coat. Set aside.

three Blanch the cabbage leaves in lightly salted boiling water for 30 seconds, then drain and refresh under cold water. Pat dry with paper towels.

four Arrange the cabbage leaves in a bamboo steamer and carefully spoon the shrimp and their marinade on top of the leaves. Cover and steam for 2–3 minutes, or until the shrimp are pink.

five Meanwhile, heat the sesame oil in a small pan until hot. Transfer the cabbage leaves and shrimp to a serving dish, pour the sesame oil over them, and serve scattered with the herbs.

skate with sage butter

1 large skate wing
4 tbsp. unsalted butter
2 tbsp. chopped sage
4 tbsp. capers in brine, drained and rinsed
2 tbsp. balsamic vinegar
½ cup hot fish or vegetable stock
a dash of lemon juice
salt and pepper

one Wash and dry the skate wing and cut as evenly as possible into 4 portions. Season lightly with salt and pepper. Melt 1 tbsp. of the butter in a large frying pan and sauté the skate for 4–5 minutes on each side, or until just browned. Remove from the heat and keep warm.

two Wipe out the frying pan and melt the remaining butter. When it stops foaming, add the sage leaves and sauté until golden. Stir in the capers, vinegar, and stock and simmer until reduced slightly.

three Season to taste with salt, pepper, and lemon juice. Drizzle the sage butter over the skate and serve immediately.

Preparation time 10 minutes Cooking time 20 minutes Total time 30 minutes Serves 4

swordfish ciabatta with salsa rossa

1 large red pepper, quartered and seeded
2 tbsp. extra virgin olive oil, plus extra for brushing
1 garlic clove, crushed
2 ripe tomatoes, peeled and chopped
a pinch of dried chili flakes
1 tsp. dried oregano
1 large ciabatta
4 thinly cut swordfish steaks, about 3½ oz. each
salt and pepper
salad greens, to serve
lemon wedges, to garnish

A steak sandwich with a healthy difference. Ask your fishmonger to cut the swordfish into ¼ in. slices.

one Place the red pepper under a preheated broiler and cook for 3–4 minutes on each side, until charred and tender. Transfer to a plastic bag and set aside to cool for 5 minutes.

two Meanwhile, heat half the oil in a small pan and sauté the garlic for 30 seconds. Add the tomatoes, chili, and oregano and simmer for 5 minutes.

three Using rubber gloves to protect the hands if the pepper is still hot, peel the skin and dice the flesh. Add to the tomato mixture and cook for another 5 minutes, until the sauce is thickened. Season to taste with salt and pepper and set aside.

four While the sauce is cooking, cut the ciabatta into quarters and toast on both sides. Drizzle with oil.

five Season the swordfish steaks with salt and pepper and brush with a little oil. Sear on a very hot griddle for about 30 seconds on each side and serve on the toasted bread with a spoonful of the sauce and some salad greens. Serve garnished with lemon wedges.

Preparation time 15 minutes Total time 15 minutes Serves 4

smoked chicken and sweet mustard wraps

8 small wheat tortillas
12 oz. boneless, skinless, smoked, cooked chicken
2 slices Parma ham, cut into strips
2 tomatoes, diced
1 oz. mixed baby salad greens
a handful of fresh herb leaves (such as basil, mint, and parsley)
salt and pepper

Sweet mustard dressing
4 tbsp. extra virgin olive oil
1 tbsp. wholegrain mustard
1 tsp. white wine vinegar
½ tsp. sugar

one Warm the tortillas according to package instructions, cover with a clean dishtowel and set aside.

two Shred the cooked chicken. Mix the chicken, ham, and tomatoes with the salad greens and herbs.

three Whisk all the dressing ingredients together, toss with the smoked chicken, and season to taste with salt and pepper. Divide between the tortillas, wrap, and serve.

Preparation time 15 minutes Cooking time 5 minutes, plus resting Total time 23 minutes Serves 4

warm tea-smoked salmon salad with wilted arugula

1 quantity Smoke Mix (see page 9)
4 salmon fillets, about 4 oz. each
4 oz. cherry tomatoes, halved
4 oz. arugula leaves

Dressing
1 shallot, finely chopped
1 garlic clove, finely chopped
a few thyme sprigs
1 tsp. Dijon mustard
2 tsp. white wine vinegar
4–5 tbsp. extra virgin olive oil
salt and pepper

Although smoking fish and meat over a mixture of tea leaves, sugar, and rice is a method widely used in Chinese cooking, this dish adopts the method for a more European combination. You will need a wok with a lid and a trivet for this recipe.

one Line a wok with a large sheet of foil, allowing it to overhang the edges, and pour in the smoke mix. Place a trivet over the top. Cover with a tight-fitting lid and heat for 5 minutes, or until the mixture is smoking.

two Meanwhile, remove any remaining bones from the salmon with a pair of tweezers. Place the tomatoes in a bowl with the arugula leaves.

three Quickly remove the lid from the wok and place the salmon fillets, skin-side down, on the trivet. Cover and cook over high heat for 5 minutes. Remove from the heat and set aside, covered, for another 3 minutes.

four Meanwhile, make the dressing. Put the shallots, garlic, thyme leaves, mustard, vinegar, and oil in a bowl and season to taste with salt and pepper. Whisk well to combine.

five Flake the salmon into the salad, add the dressing, and toss well. Serve immediately.

Preparation time 25 minutes Cooking time 3 minutes Total time 28 minutes Serves 4

fresh crab and mango salad

1 small egg yolk
1 tsp. Dijon mustard
1 tbsp. fresh lemon juice
8 tbsp. extra virgin olive oil
8 oz. fresh crab meat
1 red chili, seeded and chopped
4 oz. small green beans
1 small mango
1 head endive
2 tbsp. chopped cilantro
salt and pepper

one Whisk the egg yolk, mustard, and lemon juice until frothy and then slowly whisk in 5 tbsp. of the oil. Season with salt and pepper.

two Carefully pick through the crab to remove any small pieces of shell or cartilage. Stir the chili into the crab meat with the dressing.

three Blanch the beans in lightly salted boiling water for 3 minutes. Drain and refresh under cold water, then pat dry with paper towels. Peel the mango and then thinly slice the flesh from the pit. Separate the endive into spears. Arrange the chicory, mango, beans, and crab on serving plates.

four In a food processor or blender, process the remaining oil with the cilantro leaves and a little salt to make a fresh green dressing. Pour around the salad and serve.

Preparation time 13 minutes Cooking time 17 minutes Total time 30 minutes Serves 4

mussel and lemon pasta

12 oz. dried spaghetti
2 lb. mussels
6 tbsp. extra virgin olive oil
2 garlic cloves, sliced
1 large red chili, seeded and chopped
grated rind and juice of 1 lemon
4 tbsp. chopped cilantro
salt and pepper

Use a wok or large frying pan to sauté the garlic mixture, as everything is heated through together just before serving.

one Cook the pasta in a large pan of lightly salted boiling water for 10 minutes, until tender but still firm to the bite. Drain and reserve.

two While the pasta is cooking, scrub and debeard the mussels. Discard any that are broken or do not shut immediately when sharply tapped with the back of a knife. Set aside.

three Heat the oil in a wok or frying pan and sauté the garlic, chilies, and lemon rind, stirring occasionally, for 3 minutes or until golden. Remove from the heat.

four Put the mussels into a large saucepan with 2 tbsp. water, cover tightly, and cook, shaking the pan frequently, for 4 minutes, or until the shells have opened. Discard any mussels that remain closed.

five Return the garlic mixture to the heat and stir in the pasta, the mussels and their cooking liquid, the lemon juice, and the cilantro. Season to taste with salt and pepper, heat through and serve.

Preparation time 7 minutes Total time 7 minutes Serves 2

cucumber and mint refresher

1 cucumber
2 tbsp. chopped mint
1 cup yogurt
2 tbsp. rosewater
2 tsp. honey
ice cubes, to serve
mint sprigs, to decorate

one Peel the cucumber and cut in half lengthwise. Scoop out the seeds and chop the flesh coarsely. Put the chopped mint in a blender with the cucumber, yogurt, rosewater, and honey. Process until smooth and flecked with green.

two Put some ice cubes into glasses and top off with the cucumber drink. Decorate with mint sprigs.

Preparation time 10–12 minutes Total time 10–12 minutes Serves 4

chilled peach zinger

4 ripe peaches
1 tbsp. citrus cordial
juice of 1 lime
crushed ice
1 cup lemonade

Add a shot of vodka during step 2 for an alcoholic version.

one Plunge the peaches in boiling water for 1–2 minutes. Refresh in cold water and peel off the skins. Halve, pit, and coarsely chop the flesh.

two Place the peaches, cordial, and lime juice in a blender and process to a smooth purée.

three Half-fill 4 tall glasses with crushed ice, add the peach purée, and top off with lemonade.

midweek meals

When friends are coming over midweek, I like to pick up a few fresh ingredients on my way home to add to those in my cupboards and throw together a yummy supper without having to get too stressed by it all. Quite often, with a little organization, I manage to prepare a starter, main course, and a dessert in no time at all.

Preparation time 8 minutes Cooking time 12 minutes Total time 20 minutes Serves 4

fresh pea and tomato frittata

4 oz. fresh or frozen peas
2 tbsp. extra virgin olive oil
1 bunch scallions, sliced
1 garlic clove, crushed
4 oz. cherry tomatoes, halved
6 eggs
2 tbsp. chopped mint
a handful pea shoots (optional)
salt and pepper
arugula leaves and shavings of Parmesan cheese, to serve (optional)

one If using fresh peas, cook the peas in a pan of lightly salted boiling water for 3 minutes. Drain and refresh under cold water.

two Heat the oil in a nonstick frying pan and sauté the scallions and garlic for 2 minutes, then add the tomatoes and peas.

three Beat the eggs with the mint and season with salt and pepper. Swirl the egg mixture into the pan, scatter over the pea shoots, and cook over medium heat for 3–4 minutes, or until almost set.

four Transfer to a preheated broiler and cook for 2–3 minutes longer, or until lightly browned and cooked through. Cool slightly and serve in wedges with the arugula and Parmesan shavings, if desired.

Preparation time 10 minutes Cooking time 20 minutes Total time 30 minutes Serves 6

pumpkin and coconut soup

2 tbsp. sunflower oil
1 onion, chopped
4 garlic cloves, crushed
1 in. piece of fresh ginger, peeled and grated
2 red chilies, seeded and chopped
1 tsp. ground coriander
½ tsp. ground cumin
seeds from 2 cardamom pods
1½ lb. pumpkin, peeled and diced
2½ cups vegetable stock
½ cup coconut milk
1 tbsp. tamarind pulp
1 cinnamon stick, lightly crushed
2 tbsp. chopped cilantro
salt and pepper

To serve
cilantro leaves
yogurt
naan bread

one Heat the oil in a large saucepan and sauté the onion, garlic, ginger, chilies, and spices, stirring frequently, for 10 minutes.

two Add the pumpkin, stock, coconut milk, tamarind pulp, and cinnamon and bring to a boil. Lower the heat, cover, and simmer gently for about 10 minutes, or just until the pumpkin is tender.

three Discard the cinnamon and process the soup with the chopped cilantro in a food processor or blender until smooth. Transfer the soup to bowls, garnish with cilantro leaves and yogurt, and serve with naan bread.

sweet potato, olive, and fontina panini

8 oz. sweet potato, thinly sliced
1 tbsp. extra virgin olive oil
vegetable oil, for frying
12 sage leaves
1 ciabatta
2 tbsp. olive paste
8 oz. fontina cheese, thinly sliced
salt and pepper
green salad, to serve

A really tasty toasted sandwich. To serve 4, double the quantities below. You will probably need to grill the bread in batches unless you have 2 grill pans or broil it in the oven.

one Brush the sweet potato slices with the olive oil and season lightly with salt and pepper. Cook on a hot griddle or grill for 3–4 minutes each side, or until charred and tender. Clean the griddle.

two Meanwhile, heat a little vegetable oil in a small frying pan and sauté the sage leaves for about 30 seconds, until crisp. Drain on paper towels.

three Cut the ciabatta into quarters and then trim these so that all 4 pieces will fit on to the griddle. Heat the griddle and brush with a little oil. Cook the ciabatta pieces, cut-side down, for 1 minute, or until toasted.

four Spread the toasted sides of the ciabatta with olive paste and sandwich together with layers of cheese, sage leaves, and the potato slices.

five Grill the whole sandwiches for 1–2 minutes on each side, or until toasted and the cheese in the middle is melting. Serve with a green salad.

chicken, taleggio, and prosciutto melt

4 skinless chicken breast fillets
4 slices prosciutto
4 oz. taleggio or Camembert cheese
extra virgin olive oil, for brushing
balsamic vinegar, for drizzling
salt and pepper
tomato, olive, and basil salad, to serve

Butterflied chicken breast fillets are stuffed with taleggio, an Italian soft cows' milk cheese, and prosciutto and then pan-fried until melted and gooey—delicious!

one Using a sharp knife, slice horizontally through the thicker side of the chicken breast fillets without cutting all the way through. Open up and season with salt and pepper.

two Lay a slice of ham in each breast. Slice the cheese into 4 and add to the ham. Fold the chicken over to enclose the filling.

three Brush each chicken breast with a little oil and cook on a hot griddle pan for 8–10 minutes on each side, until browned and cooked through, and the cheese is oozing from the middle.

four Serve the chicken drizzled with a little balsamic vinegar, more oil, and a tomato, olive and basil salad.

Preparation time 15 minutes Cooking time 15 minutes Total time 30 minutes Serves 4

mussels with lemon curry sauce

2 lb. mussels, scrubbed and debearded
½ cup Indian beer
1 tbsp. unsalted butter
1 onion, chopped
1 garlic clove, crushed
1 in. piece of fresh ginger, peeled and grated
1 tbsp. medium curry powder
½ cup light cream
2 tbsp. lemon juice
salt and pepper
chopped parsley, to garnish
crusty bread, to serve

one Discard any mussels that are broken or do not close immediately when sharply tapped with a knife. Place them in a large pan with the beer, cover and cook, shaking the pan frequently, for 4 minutes, or until all the shells have opened. Discard any that remain closed. Strain and reserve the cooking liquid. Keep the mussels warm.

two Meanwhile, melt the butter in a large pan and sauté the onions, garlic, ginger, and curry powder, stirring frequently, for 5 minutes.

three Strain in the reserved cooking liquid and bring to a boil. Boil until reduced by half. Whisk in the cream and lemon juice and simmer gently.

four Stir in the mussels, warm through, and season to taste with salt and pepper. Garnish with chopped parsley and serve with crusty bread.

Preparation time 10 minutes Cooking time 10 minutes Total time 20 minutes Serves 4

smoked haddock, poached eggs, and caper butter

4 smoked haddock fillets, about 6 oz. each
4 eggs
4 tbsp. softened unsalted butter
2 tbsp. capers in brine, drained and rinsed
6 dill sprigs
salt and pepper

one Put the haddock into a frying pan, skin-side up, cover with cold water, and bring to a boil. Poach for 5 minutes, then remove with a slotted spoon, and drain on paper towels. Set aside and keep warm. Reserve the fish cooking liquid.

two Crack the eggs into the cooking liquid and poach for 2–3 minutes.

three Melt the butter in a frying pan until foaming. Add the capers and dill and sauté until the butter starts to turn brown. Season to taste with salt and pepper.

four Top each haddock fillet with a poached egg and serve drizzled with the caper butter.

stir-fried beef with noodles

2 tbsp. dark soy sauce
2 tsp. honey
1 lb. thick sirloin steak, very thinly sliced
2 oz. cashew nuts
6 oz. flat rice noodles
2 tbsp. sunflower oil
1 tsp. sesame oil
1 garlic clove, chopped
1 fresh red chili, seeded and chopped
1 red pepper, seeded and sliced
¼ cup hot beef stock
1 tbsp. Thai fish sauce
2 tbsp. lime juice
4 tbsp. chopped basil

one Combine the soy sauce and honey in a large dish. Add the beef and turn to coat. Set aside to marinate for 10 minutes, then drain the beef, reserving the marinade.

two Meanwhile, toast the cashews, then coarsely chop them.

three Soak the noodles according to the package instructions, then drain and set aside.

four Heat the two oils in a wok, add the garlic, chili, and red pepper and stir-fry for 30 seconds. Add the beef and stir-fry for another 2 minutes.

five Add the noodles, reserved marinade, beef stock, fish sauce, and lime juice and cook for 2 minutes. Add the basil and serve topped with the cashews.

Preparation time 10 minutes Cooking time 12 minutes Total time 22 minutes Serves 4

garlicky shrimp and basil pasta

12 oz. dried fusilli
2 garlic cloves
1 oz. pine nuts
6 tbsp. extra virgin olive oil
pinch of dried chili flakes
12 oz. cooked peeled tiger shrimp
juice of ½ lemon
1 oz. chopped basil leaves
salt and pepper

Choose large, cooked peeled shrimp for this dish. Do not overcook them as they need only to be heated through and can become tough if cooked for too long.

one Cook the pasta in a large saucepan of lightly salted boiling water for 10–12 minutes until tender but still firm to the bite. Drain the pasta, reserving ¼ cup of the cooking liquid.

two Meanwhile, crush the garlic and toast the pine nuts. Heat the oil in a wok and stir-fry the garlic and chili flakes for about 30 seconds, or until starting to brown. Add the shrimp and stir-fry for 1 minute.

three Stir in the pasta, reserved cooking liquid, pine nuts, lemon juice, and basil, season to taste with salt and pepper and heat through before serving.

Preparation time 10 minutes Cooking time 12 minutes Total time 22 minutes Serves 4

pasta with fava beans and artichoke pesto

12 oz. dried penne
12 oz. frozen fava beans
3 oz. marinated charred artichokes,
coarsely chopped
1 garlic clove, chopped
½ oz. parsley, chopped
1 tbsp. pine nuts
½ oz. pecorino cheese, grated, plus
extra to serve
½ cup extra virgin olive oil
salt and pepper

Marinated charred artichokes are often sold in jars. If you can't find them, use canned artichoke hearts instead.

one Cook the pasta in a large saucepan of lightly salted, boiling water for 10–12 minutes, until tender but still firm to the bite. At the same time, blanch the fava beans in a pan of lightly salted, boiling water for 3 minutes. Drain and set aside.

two Put the artichokes, garlic, parsley, and pine nuts in a food processor and process until fairly smooth. Transfer the mixture to a bowl and stir in the pecorino and oil and season to taste with salt and pepper.

three Drain the pasta, reserving 4 tbsp. of the cooking liquid, and return it to the pan. Add the pesto mixture, fava beans, and reserved cooking liquid and season to taste with pepper. Toss over medium heat until warmed through. Serve with extra grated pecorino.

spinach and four cheese pizza

8½ oz. package pizza crust mix
1 tbsp. extra virgin olive oil
1 garlic clove, crushed
2 rosemary sprigs, chopped
7 oz. frozen spinach, thawed
4 oz. dolcelatte cheese
4 tbsp. mascarpone cheese
pinch of grated nutmeg
5 oz. mozzarella cheese, sliced
1 oz. Parmesan cheese, grated
salt and pepper

To make these pizzas successfully in 30 minutes requires organization. Read the recipe through carefully before beginning and make sure you clear plenty of work space for rolling the two crusts out.

one Put two baking sheets into a preheated 425°F oven to heat up.

two Mix up the pizza dough with the olive oil, according to the package instructions, adding the garlic and rosemary to the mix. Divide the dough in half and roll each piece out to a 14 in. round.

three Squeeze out all the excess liquid from the spinach and beat in the dolcelatte and mascarpone. Season to taste with grated nutmeg, salt, and pepper.

four Place one pizza crust on a well-floured board and top with half the spinach mixture, half the mozzarella, and half the Parmesan. Season to taste with salt and pepper and carefully slide on to one of the heated baking sheets. Repeat to make the second pizza and slide on to the second baking sheet.

five Bake for 12 minutes or until cooked, swapping the pizzas half-way through so that they brown evenly. To serve, cut each pizza in half and serve immediately.

spring green and goat cheese risotto

4 tbsp. extra virgin olive oil
2 leeks, sliced
2 garlic cloves, chopped
8 oz. arborio rice
½ cup dry white wine
4 cups hot vegetable stock
8 oz. broccoli, cut into florets
8 oz. baby spinach, shredded
1 oz. chopped mixed herbs (such as basil, chives, mint, parsley, and tarragon)
4 oz. soft goat cheese, mashed
2 oz. Parmesan cheese, grated
salt and pepper

The cooking method here may seem strange to risotto purists, but as time is limited, I've had to make a few short cuts. Although not strictly authentic, this combination is still totally delicious.

one Heat the oil in a large saucepan and sauté the leeks and garlic for 1 minute. Add the rice and stir for 30 seconds, or until all the grains are glossy. Add the wine, bring to a boil, and cook until almost all the liquid has evaporated.

two Gradually add the stock, a ladleful at a time, stirring frequently for 18 minutes or until almost all the stock is absorbed. Add the broccoli to the rice after 12 minutes.

three Stir the spinach, herbs and both cheeses into the rice with the remaining stock. Season to taste with salt and pepper and cook for a final 2 minutes until the spinach is wilted. Serve immediately.

Preparation time 8 minutes Cooking time 22 minutes Total time 30 minutes Serves 4

ham steaks with creamy lentils

4 oz. Puy lentils
2 tbsp. butter
2 shallots
1 garlic clove, chopped
2 thyme sprigs, crushed
1 tsp. cumin seeds
4 tsp. Dijon mustard
2 tsp. honey
4 ham steaks
½ cup dry cider
6 tbsp. light cream
salt and pepper
thyme leaves, to garnish

one Place the lentils in a pan and cover with cold water. Bring to a boil and cook for 20 minutes.

two Meanwhile, melt the butter in a frying pan and sauté the shallots, garlic, thyme, and cumin seeds, stirring frequently, for 10 minutes, or until the shallots are soft and golden.

three Blend the mustard and honey and season to taste with salt and pepper. Brush the mixture over the ham steaks and grill for 3 minutes on each side, or until golden and cooked through. Keep warm.

four Drain the lentils and add them to the shallot mixture. Pour in the cider, bring to a boil, and cook until reduced to about 4 tbsp. Stir in the cream, heat through, and season to taste with salt and pepper. Serve with the ham steaks garnished with thyme leaves.

Preparation time 5 minutes Cooking time 23 minutes Total time 28 minutes Serves 4

pork steaks with apples and mustard mashed potatoes

4 medium baking potatoes, peeled and diced
1 large green apple, peeled, cored, and quartered
a handful sage leaves, chopped
2 tbsp. extra virgin olive oil
1 tbsp. lemon juice
1 tbsp. honey
4 pork steaks, 7 oz. each
2 tbsp. butter
2 tbsp. milk
1 tbsp. Dijon mustard
salt and pepper

one Cook the potatoes in a saucepan of lightly salted boiling water for 10 minutes, or until tender.

two Cut the apple quarters into thick wedges. Mix the sage with the oil, lemon juice, and honey and season to taste with salt and pepper. Mix half the flavored oil with the apple wedges. Brush the rest over the pork steaks.

three Grill the steaks for 3–4 minutes on each side, until browned and cooked through. Set aside and keep warm.

four Drain the potatoes, mash and beat in 1½ tbsp. of the butter, the milk, and mustard and season to taste with salt and pepper. Keep warm.

five Melt the remaining butter in a frying pan and quickly sauté the apple wedges for 2–3 minutes, until golden and softened. Serve the pork with the mustard mashed potatoes, apples, and any pork juices.

Preparation time 2 minutes Cooking time 4 minutes Total time 6 minutes Serves 4

bananas with palm sugar toffee sauce

4 bananas
4 tbsp. unsalted butter
½ cup palm sugar
½ cup heavy cream
dash of lime juice
vanilla ice cream, to serve
ground cinnamon or grated nutmeg,
to decorate (optional)

one Peel the bananas and cut into quarters or in half lengthwise. Melt the butter in a frying pan and sauté the banana halves for about 30 seconds on each side, or until lightly golden. Transfer to a warm dish with a slotted spoon.

two Stir the sugar and cream into the pan and heat gently to dissolve the sugar. Simmer gently for 2–3 minutes, until thickened. Add lime juice to taste.

three Serve the bananas drizzled with the toffee sauce and with a scoop of ice cream. Sprinkle with cinnamon or nutmeg to decorate, if desired.

Preparation time 7 minutes Cooking time 13 minutes Total time 20 minutes Serves 4

instant apple crumbles with custard

2 lb. Bramley apples, peeled, cored, and
thickly sliced
1 tbsp. butter
2 tbsp. sugar
1 tbsp. lemon juice
2 tbsp. water

Custard
1 cup milk
3 egg yolks
1 tbsp. sugar
a few drops vanilla extract

Crumble
2 tbsp. butter
3 oz. fresh wholewheat breadcrumbs
1 oz. pumpkin seeds
2 tbsp. soft brown sugar

This is not strictly a crumble—the apples are stewed and then topped with crispy crumbs and toasted pumpkin seeds and served with homemade custard. It tastes almost the same as the real thing and is truly delicious.

one Place the apples in a saucepan with the butter, sugar, lemon juice, and water. Cover and simmer for 8–10 minutes, until softened but still holding some shape.

two Meanwhile, make the custard. Heat the milk to boiling, then remove from the heat. Beat the egg yolks and sugar together, stir in the hot milk, and return to the pan. Stir over low heat until thickened. Stir in the vanilla and keep warm.

three Melt the butter for the crumble in a frying pan and stir-fry the breadcrumbs until lightly golden, then add the pumpkin seeds and stir-fry for 1 minute longer. Remove from the heat and stir in the sugar.

four Spoon the apple mixture into bowls, sprinkle over the crumble, and serve with the custard.

two's company

Perfect for a romantic evening in or for a tête-à-tête meal. Many cookbooks cater to four to six servings, but I often end up cooking for myself and one friend, so these dishes all serve two. Of course, if you desire to make any of them for more people, simply multiply the ingredients accordingly.

Preparation time 5 minutes Cooking time 17 minutes Total time 22 minutes Serves 2

pasta with radicchio and cheese crumbs

6 oz. dried spaghetti
2½ tbsp. butter
1 oz. fresh white breadcrumbs
½ oz. Parmesan cheese, grated
2 shallots, finely chopped
1 garlic clove, sliced
1 head radicchio, shredded
dash of lemon juice
salt and pepper

one Cook the pasta in a large pan of lightly salted boiling water for 10–12 minutes, until tender but still firm to the bite. Drain the pasta, reserving 2 tbsp. of the cooking liquid.

two Meanwhile, melt half the butter in a frying pan and sauté the breadcrumbs, stirring frequently, for about 5 minutes, or until evenly golden and crisp. Transfer the crumbs to a bowl, cool slightly, and add the Parmesan.

three Heat the remaining butter in a wok or large saucepan and sauté the shallots and garlic, stirring occasionally, for 5 minutes, until softened. Add the radicchio to the pan with a little lemon juice and season to taste with salt and pepper. Stir over low heat for about 2 minutes, or until the radicchio has wilted. Add the pasta, toss until heated through, and serve topped with the cheese crumbs.

Preparation time 10 minutes Cooking time 15 minutes Total time 25 minutes Serves 2

pasta primavera

12 oz. mixed summer vegetables (such as baby carrots, small string beans, zucchini, and fennel)
8 oz. dried spaghetti
2 tbsp. extra virgin olive oil
1 shallot, finely chopped
1 garlic clove, sliced
½ cup dry white wine
¾ cup plus 1 tbsp. light cream
2 tbsp. chopped mixed herbs (such as chervil, chives, mint, and parsley)
1 oz. Parmesan cheese, grated
salt and pepper

one Trim and slice the vegetables as necessary and plunge into a large pan of lightly salted boiling water and blanch for 2 minutes. Drain, reserving the cooking liquid, and refresh the vegetables in cold water.

two Bring the vegetable water back to a boil, add the pasta, and cook for 10–12 minutes, until tender but still firm to the bite. Drain and reserve.

three Meanwhile, heat the oil in a wok or large frying pan and sauté the shallot and garlic for 5 minutes. Add the vegetables and cook for another minute.

four Add the wine, bring to a boil, and cook until reduced by half. Add the cream and herbs and bring back to a boil. Stir in the spaghetti and Parmesan and season to taste with salt and pepper. Heat through and serve.

Preparation time 10 minutes Cooking time 20 minutes Total time 30 minutes Serves 2

seafood fondue

1 lemongrass stalk, finely shredded
4 lime leaves, finely shredded
2 garlic cloves, chopped
1 in. piece of fresh ginger, peeled and grated
4 small red chilies, seeded and chopped
4 cups fish stock
2 tbsp. Thai fish sauce
1 tbsp. light soy sauce
1 tbsp. palm sugar
juice of 1 lime
4 oz. egg thread noodles
6 large raw shrimp, peeled and
deveined (see page 33)
4 prepared baby squid, sliced into rings
6 scallops
2 oz. bean sprouts
a large handful herb sprigs
(such as basil, cilantro, and mint)

This is an Asian seafood dish where the stock is brought to the table in a special pot called a steamboat and the raw ingredients are served on a platter, so you can poach them in the stock yourself, much as you would with a fondue. You can either use a fondue pot or buy a steamboat from a well-stocked kitchen shop or Asian specialty store. Alternatively, cook the stock on the burner and serve in bowls.

one Place the lemongrass, lime leaves, garlic, ginger, chilies, stock, fish sauce, soy sauce, sugar, and lime juice in a saucepan. Bring to a boil, cover, and simmer for 20 minutes.

two Meanwhile, soak the noodles in hot water, according to package instructions, then drain and refresh under cold water. Butterfly the shrimp (see page 33); and slice the squid into rings.

three Transfer the hot stock to a Chinese steamboat or a fondue pot and light the burner. Arrange the raw seafood, bean sprouts, noodles, and herbs on a platter and bring to the table so that each person can cook their own food in the hot stock.

deep-fried tofu with stir-fried vegetables

vegetable oil, for deep-frying
8 oz. firm tofu, cut into cubes
2 tbsp. sunflower oil
1 garlic clove, sliced
8 oz. broccoli, cut into florets
4 oz. French beans, halved
2 carrots, thinly sliced
½ cup hot vegetable stock
3 tbsp. oyster sauce
2 tbsp. brown sugar
2 tbsp. sweet chili sauce
4 oz. bean sprouts
2 tbsp. chopped mint
cooked rice, to serve

one Heat the oil for deep-frying and fry the tofu for 2–3 minutes, until crisp and golden. Drain on paper towels and keep warm.

two Heat the sunflower oil in a wok and sauté the garlic for 1 minute. Remove with a slotted spoon and discard. Add the broccoli, beans, and carrots and stir-fry for 3 minutes.

three Combine the stock, oyster sauce, sugar, and chili sauce and add to the pan. Cook for 2–3 minutes, until the vegetables are tender. Stir in the bean sprouts and mint and serve with the tofu and some cooked rice.

malay chicken noodles

2 garlic cloves
2 tbsp. sunflower oil
1 fresh red chili, seeded and finely chopped
2 shallots, thinly sliced
2 skinless chicken breast fillets, thinly sliced
1 in. piece of fresh ginger, peeled and grated
¼ tsp. ground coriander
4 oz. thin rice noodles
2 oz. snow peas, halved
1 red pepper, seeded and sliced
1 oz. bean sprouts
3 tbsp. kecap manis or soy sauce
1 tbsp. Thai fish sauce
1 tbsp. medium dry sherry
1 tbsp. lemon juice
chopped cilantro, to garnish

one Slice 1 garlic clove and crush the other. Heat the oil in a wok and stir-fry the sliced garlic, chili, and shallots for about 3 minutes, until golden and starting to crisp, but do not allow them to burn. Drain with a slotted spoon and reserve. Remove the wok from the heat, reserving the oil.

two Toss together the chicken breast, ginger, crushed garlic, and ground coriander in a bowl. Soak the noodles in hot water, according to the package instructions, then drain and reserve.

three Reheat the oil in the wok and add the chicken mixture. Stir-fry for 3 minutes, until golden. Add the snow peas, red pepper, and bean sprouts, and stir-fry for another minute.

four Finally, add the noodles, kecap manis or soy sauce, fish sauce, sherry, and lemon juice and cook for 1–2 minutes, until heated through. Serve topped with the shallot mixture and chopped cilantro.

Preparation time 12 minutes Cooking time 11 minutes Total time 23 minutes Serves 2

steamed chicken with bok choy and ginger

½ in. piece of fresh ginger, peeled and grated
1 small garlic clove, crushed
1 tbsp. dark soy sauce
1 tbsp. tangerine syrup
1½ tsp. mirin
1 tsp. sugar
pinch of Chinese five-spice powder
2 skinless chicken breast fillets
2 bok choy, halved
cilantro, to garnish

Ginger salsa
1 in. piece of stem ginger, peeled and very finely shredded
1 red chili, seeded and finely chopped
a few cilantro leaves, chopped
1 tsp. sesame oil
juice of ½ lime
salt and pepper

one Combine the ginger, garlic, soy sauce, tangerine syrup, mirin, sugar, and five-spice powder in a bowl. Place the chicken in a shallow, heatproof dish, pour in the mixture, and turn to coat. Set aside to marinate for 10 minutes.

two Meanwhile, make the ginger salsa. Mix together the stem ginger, chili, cilantro leaves, sesame oil, and lime juice and season to taste with salt and pepper.

three Place the chicken with the marinade in a bamboo steamer and cook for 8 minutes. Remove the chicken from the dish and keep warm. Steam the bok choy in the cooking juices for 2–3 minutes. Serve the chicken and bok choy with the salsa, garnished with cilantro.

tea-smoked duck with roasted squash salad

8 oz. butternut squash, peeled and cut into cubes
4 tsp. olive oil
2 small duck breasts, about 7 oz. each
1 tsp. Thai seven-spice seasoning
1 quantity Smoke Mix (see page 9)
2 star anise
2 oz. frisée lettuce
1 tbsp. wild garlic chives or chives
salt and pepper

Dressing
1 in. piece of fresh ginger, peeled and grated
1 tbsp. rice vinegar
pinch of dried chili flakes
4 tbsp. sunflower oil

one Toss the squash with 3 tsp. of the oil in a roasting pan or ovenproof dish. Season to taste with salt and pepper. Roast in a preheated 425°F oven for 20 minutes or until the squash is golden.

two Meanwhile, brush the duck breasts with the remaining oil and rub with 1 tsp. salt and the seven-spice mix.

three Line a wok with 1–2 sheets of foil, making sure the foil is touching the base of the wok. Add the smoke mix and the star anise, and place a trivet over the top. Lay the duck breasts on the trivet, cover with a tight-fitting lid, and smoke over medium heat for 12 minutes. Remove the wok from the heat and set aside, still covered, for an additional 5 minutes.

four To make the dressing, mix the ginger, vinegar, chili flakes, and sunflower oil.

five Put the frisée and wild garlic chives or chives into a bowl, add the squash and dressing, and toss to mix. Cut the duck breasts in half or into slices and serve with the salad.

pork escalopes with creamy herb sauce

8 oz. pork tenderloin
2 tbsp. butter
1 garlic clove, crushed
grated rind of ½ lemon
4 tbsp. chopped mixed herbs (such as chervil, chives, parsley, and tarragon)
¼ cup. Pernod
4 tbsp. heavy cream
salt and pepper
tagliatelle, to serve

This is a lovely quick and simple supper dish, full of rich flavors and creamy textures. I think it is best served with good-quality egg pasta.

one Cut the pork into ¼ in. thick slices and place between layers of plastic wrap. Beat with a meat mallet or rolling pin until doubled in size.

two Melt the butter in a large frying pan. When it stops foaming, add the pork slices and cook for 30 seconds on each side, or until browned. Add the garlic, lemon rind, and herbs and cook for 1 minute.

three Add the Pernod and cook until reduced by half. Stir in the cream, season to taste with salt and pepper, and heat through. Serve immediately with tagliatelle.

Preparation time 5 minutes, plus infusing **Cooking time** 15 minutes **Total time** 20 minutes **Serves** 2

sweet bruschetta with sauternes custard

1 tbsp. unsalted butter
1 egg
few drops vanilla extract
2 tbsp. sugar
½ cup milk
4 slices white bread, crusts removed
raspberries, to serve

Sauternes custard
7 tablespoons heavy cream
2 tbsp. Sauternes wine
½ vanilla pod
2 egg yolks
1 tbsp. sugar

This dish reminds me of bread and butter pudding, but here it is cooked like French Toast, making it lighter than the more traditional English pudding.

one First, make the custard. Heat the cream, wine, and vanilla pod to the boiling point. Remove the pan from the heat and set aside to infuse for 10 minutes.

two Beat the egg yolks and sugar together, strain in the infused cream, and return to the pan. Heat gently, stirring constantly until thickened. Do not allow the mixture to boil. Remove the pan from the heat and keep warm.

three Melt the butter in a frying pan. Meanwhile, beat the egg with the vanilla extract, sugar, and milk in a shallow bowl. Dip in the bread slices and sauté in the butter for 1–2 minutes on each side, or until crisp and lightly golden. Serve topped with raspberries and pass the custard separately.

fruit and mascarpone gratin

2 oz. mixed fruits and berries (such as peach, strawberries, raspberries and blueberries)
2 oz. mascarpone cheese
1 egg yolk
1 oz. sugar
1 tbsp. Amaretto di Saronno

Amaretto is an Italian liqueur made from apricot kernels.

one Prepare the fruits and arrange in a single layer on 2 heatproof plates or in individual gratin dishes.

two Beat the mascarpone, egg yolk, sugar and Amaretto together until smooth and then spoon over the fruits.

three Cook under a preheated broiler for about 3 minutes, until the sauce is caramelized and the fruits are softened.

champagne and raspberry framboise

1 oz. ripe raspberries
1 tbsp. Framboise
½ bottle chilled champagne

An ideal champagne cocktail to get the evening off to a bubbly start.

one Mix the raspberries with the Framboise and chill for 15 minutes.

two Spoon into cocktail glasses or flutes and top up with the champagne.

summer berry sorbet

8 oz. frozen mixed summer berries
6 tablespoons spiced berry cordial
2 tbsp. Kirsch
1 tbsp. lime juice

This is not a true sorbet, but a cheat's version. Frozen summer berries are blended with fruit cordial for an instant ice.

one Put a shallow plastic container into the freezer to chill. Process the frozen berries, cordial, Kirsch, and lime juice in a food processor or blender until a smooth purée is reached. Be careful not to over-process, as this will soften the mixture too much.

two Spoon into the chilled container and freeze for at least 25 minutes. Spoon into bowls and serve.

fruit fritters with ice cream

½ tbsp. unsalted butter
6 tablespoons all-purpose flour
pinch of ground pumpkin pie spice
pinch of salt
1 egg, separated
6 tablespoons sparkling mineral water
4 oz. fresh fruit
sunflower oil, for deep-frying
sugar, for dusting
vanilla ice cream, to serve

Choose ripe but firm fruit for these fritters—the best fruits to use are stone fruits, such as peaches, apricots, and nectarines, but you can use apples or even bananas.

one Melt the butter in a small pan. Sift the flour, spice, and salt into a bowl. Beat in the egg yolk, melted butter, and water to make a fairly smooth batter.

two Whisk the egg white in a separate bowl and fold into the batter.

three Heat 2 in. of oil in a deep pan. Meanwhile, peel, pit, and quarter the fruit, as necessary.

four Dip the prepared fruit into the batter and deep-fry for 1–2 minutes, or until crisp and golden. Drain on paper towels.

five Dust the fritters with a little sugar and serve with a scoop of ice cream.

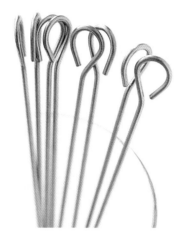

outdoor eating

There is definitely something magical about eating *al fresco*, even if, like me, you have only a small terrace. Barbecues simply epitomize summer evenings and many of the recipes in this chapter are cooked over hot coals. You'll also find several dishes ideal for picnics, so allow the food to cool, then wrap it well and transport as necessary.

Preparation time 10 minutes Cooking time 12–14 minutes Total time 22–24 minutes Serves 4

indian spiced pumpkin wedges with coconut pesto

2 lb. pumpkin
1 tsp. cumin seeds
1 tsp. coriander seeds
2 cardamom pods
3 tbsp. sunflower oil
1 tsp. sugar or mango chutney

Coconut pesto
1 oz. cilantro leaves
1 garlic clove, crushed
1 green chili, seeded and chopped
pinch of sugar
1 tbsp. shelled pistachio nuts, coarsely chopped
6 tbsp. coconut cream
1 tbsp. lime juice
salt and pepper

Creamy coconut pesto makes a perfect foil to the soft, nutty, wedges of grilled pumpkin dusted with curry spices.

one Cut the pumpkin into thin wedges about ½ in. thick and place in a large dish. Dry-fry the whole spices until browned, then grind to a powder in a spice grinder. Mix with the oil and sugar or mango chutney and toss with the pumpkin wedges to coat.

two Cook the wedges either over hot coals or under the broiler for 6–8 minutes on each side, or until charred and tender.

three Meanwhile, make the pesto. Put the cilantro leaves, garlic, chili, sugar, and nuts into a food processor. Process until fairly finely ground and blended. Season to taste with salt and pepper. Add the coconut cream and lime juice and process again. Transfer to a serving bowl and serve with the pumpkin wedges.

Preparation time 12–15 minutes Cooking time 15 minutes Total time 27–30 minutes Serves 4

mushroom parcels with melting cheese

12 flat mushrooms
2 garlic cloves, crushed
1 tsp. chopped thyme
dash of lemon juice
4 tbsp. softened butter
2 oz. pecorino cheese, grated
salt and pepper
crusty bread, to serve

one Divide the mushrooms between 4 large pieces of foil. Beat the garlic, thyme, and lemon juice into the butter and season to taste with salt and pepper. Dot the flavored butter over the mushrooms.

two Seal the foil to form packets and cook over hot coals or in a preheated 400°F oven for 10–15 minutes.

three Open the parcels, sprinkle over the cheese and allow to melt slightly, then serve with crusty bread.

Preparation time 5 minutes Cooking time 15–20 minutes Total time 20–25 minutes Serves 4

lemon and herb grilled chicken wings

2 garlic cloves, crushed
grated rind and juice of 1 lemon
4 thyme sprigs
6 tbsp. extra virgin olive oil
1 tbsp. honey
1 tsp. dried oregano
1 tsp. ground cumin
12 chicken wings
salt and pepper

one Put the garlic, lemon rind, and juice into a bowl. Add the thyme leaves, oil, honey, oregano, and cumin and season to taste with salt and pepper.

two Add the chicken wings and stir until well coated.

three Grill or broil the chicken wings for 15–20 minutes, turning and basting, until charred and cooked through.

Preparation time 4 minutes Cooking time 6 minutes Total time 10 minutes, plus cooling Serves 4

smoked ham and brie frittata

6 large free-range eggs
2 tbsp. chopped parsley
2 tbsp. extra virgin olive oil
4 oz. piece smoked ham or gammon
3 oz. Brie cheese
salt and pepper
tomato salad, to serve

one Beat together the eggs and parsley and season to taste with salt and pepper. Heat the oil in a nonstick frying pan and swirl in the egg mixture.

two Cook over medium heat for 3 minutes, until almost set. Meanwhile, shred the ham and thinly slice the Brie.

three Scatter the ham and cheese over the frittata and cook under a preheated broiler for 2–3 minutes, until golden and set. Allow to cool slightly and serve with a tomato salad.

Preparation time 5 minutes, plus marinating Cooking time 6–8 minutes

Total time 26–28 minutes Serves 2–4

eggplant steaks with miso

2 medium eggplant
1 tbsp. peanut oil
1 tbsp. dark soy sauce, plus extra
to serve
1 tbsp. balsamic vinegar
1 tbsp. wholegrain barley miso
1 tsp. stem ginger syrup (from a jar)
green salad with sesame seeds, to serve

one Cut the eggplant lengthwise into ¼ in. thick slices. Combine the oil, soy sauce, vinegar, miso, and ginger syrup and brush all over the eggplant. Set aside to marinate for 15 minutes.

two Grill or broil the eggplant, basting frequently with the marinade, for 2–4 minutes on each side, until charred and tender. Serve the eggplant with a little extra soy sauce for dipping and accompanied by a green salad scattered with sesame seeds.

Preparation time 10 minutes Cooking time 20 minutes Total time 30 minutes Serves 4

salt-crusted shrimp with chili jam

12 large raw tiger shrimp in their shells
1 tbsp. olive oil
2 oz. sea salt
lemon wedges, to garnish

Chili jam
4 ripe tomatoes
½ red onion
2 red chilies
2 tbsp. dark soy sauce
2 tbsp. honey
salt and pepper

A salt crust coats the shells of the shrimp as they cook over hot coals, leaving the flesh inside succulent and sweet. Peel the salt crust and the shells will come away too.

one First make the chili jam. Coarsely chop the tomatoes, onion, and chilies. Place in a food processor with the soy sauce and honey, season to taste with salt and pepper, and process until smooth.

two Transfer the jam to a pan and bring to a boil. Simmer rapidly for 15 minutes, or until thickened. Plunge the pan into iced water and leave to cool.

three Meanwhile, carefully cut along the back of the shrimp with a small pair of scissors and pull out the black vein. Wash and dry well.

four Toss the shrimp with the oil and then coat thoroughly with salt. Cook the shrimp in their salt jackets over hot coals or in a hot griddle pan for 2–3 minutes on each side. Serve with the chili jam and lemon wedges to garnish.

Preparation time 10 minutes Total time 10 minutes Serves 4 as a starter

watermelon and feta salad

1 tbsp. black sesame seeds
1 lb. watermelon, peeled and diced
6 oz. feta cheese, diced
2 oz. arugula leaves
a few mint, parsley, and cilantro sprigs
6 tbsp. extra virgin olive oil
1 tbsp. orange flower water
1½ tbsp. lemon juice
1 tsp. pomegranate syrup (optional)
½ tsp. sugar
salt and pepper
toasted pita bread, to serve

one Dry-fry the sesame seeds for a few minutes until aromatic, then set aside.

two Arrange the watermelon and feta on a large plate with the arugula and herbs.

three Whisk together the olive oil, orange flower water, lemon juice, pomegranate syrup, if using, and sugar, then season to taste with salt and pepper and drizzle over the salad. Scatter over the sesame seeds and serve with toasted pita bread.

Preparation time 5 minutes, plus marinating **Cooking time** 5 minutes
Total time 25 minutes **Serves** 4

chicken teriyaki with soba noodles

4 skinless chicken breast fillets
4 tbsp. dark soy sauce, plus
extra, to serve
4 tbsp. mirin
2 tbsp. sugar
8 oz. soba noodles
sesame oil, to serve

The combination of hot grilled chicken and cold noodles is exquisite.

one Cut the chicken breasts into 1 in. cubes and place in a shallow dish. Combine the soy sauce, mirin, and sugar, add to the chicken and toss well to coat. Set aside to marinate for 15 minutes.

two Meanwhile, cook the noodles according to the package instructions, then drain, refresh in iced water, drain again, and chill.

three Thread the chicken cubes on to metal skewers and grill or broil for 2–3 minutes on each side.

four Toss the noodles with a little sesame oil and serve with the chicken and extra sesame oil and soy sauce.

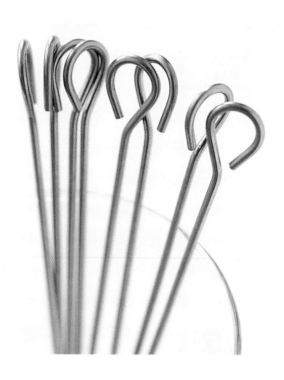

lamb cutlets with anchovies, rosemary, and lemon

juice and finely grated rind of ½ lemon
2 garlic cloves, crushed
4 rosemary sprigs, finely chopped
4 anchovy fillets in oil, drained and finely chopped
2 tbsp. extra virgin olive oil
2 tbsp. lemon cordial
12 lamb cutlets
salt and pepper
Sweet Potato Skins (see at right), to serve

To prepare sweet potato skins, cut baked sweet potatoes into quarters, scoop out some of the flesh, brush the skins with oil, season to taste with salt and pepper, and grill until crisp.

one Put the lemon rind and juice into a bowl and add the garlic, rosemary, anchovies, olive oil, and lemon cordial. Mix thoroughly and add the lamb cutlets. Season with salt and pepper, turn to coat, and set aside to marinate for 15 minutes.

two Grill or broil the lamb for 3–5 minutes on each side, until charred and cooked through. Let rest for a few minutes and serve with grilled sweet potato skins.

Preparation time 5 minutes, plus marinating Cooking time 1 minute

Total time 21 minutes Serves 4

chili steak baguette

2 tsp. chili sauce
1 tsp. honey
1 tsp. sesame oil
4–8 frying steaks, depending on the size
1 large baguette
salt and pepper

Sesame mayonnaise
½ tsp. sesame seeds
1 garlic clove, crushed
1 egg yolk
1–2 tsp. lime juice
½ cup safflower oil
1 tbsp. toasted sesame oil

The sweet-spicy coating on the steaks is perfectly balanced by the creamy mayonnaise with a hint of sesame—a sort of fusion steak sandwich.

one Combine the chili sauce, honey, and sesame oil in a small bowl and season to taste with salt and pepper. Rub the mixture all over the steaks and set aside to marinate for 15 minutes.

two Meanwhile, make the mayonnaise. Dry-fry the sesame seeds and set aside to cool. Put the garlic, egg yolk, and 1 tsp. of the lime juice into a food processor.

three Process briefly and then, with the motor running, add the oil in a steady stream through the funnel until the sauce has thickened. Season to taste with salt and pepper, stir in the sesame seeds, and add a little more lime juice, if desired.

four Grill, broil, or pan-fry the steaks for 30 seconds on each side. Cut the baguette into 4, slice and sandwich the steaks into the baguette quarters with the mayonnaise. Serve immediately.

Preparation time 10 minutes Cooking time 12 minutes Total time 22 minutes Serves 4

warm ravioli salad with beets and bitter greens

4 tbsp. extra virgin olive oil
2 red onions, thinly sliced
2 garlic cloves, thinly sliced
1 lb. fresh spinach and ricotta ravioli
12 oz. cooked beets in natural juices, drained and diced
2 tbsp. capers in brine, drained and rinsed
2 tbsp. balsamic vinegar
a few mixed bitter salad greens (such as chicory, radicchio, arugula, and frisée)
parsley sprigs
basil leaves
salt
pecorino cheese shavings, to serve (optional)

Buy the filled pasta from a store that you know sells high-quality fresh pasta. You can vary the filling as preferred.

one Heat 1 tbsp. of the oil in a large pan and sauté the onions and garlic over medium heat for 10 minutes, or until softened and golden.

two Meanwhile, cook the pasta in a pan of lightly salted boiling water, for 3 minutes, or until it is tender but still firm to the bite. Drain and toss with the remaining oil.

three Add the beets to the onions with the capers and vinegar and heat through. Stir into the ravioli and transfer to a large bowl to cool for 5 minutes, gathering in all the juices from the pan.

four Arrange the ravioli in bowls or on plates with the salad greens and herbs. Serve topped with pecorino shavings, if desired.

Preparation time 10 minutes Cooking time 15 minutes Total time 25 minutes Serves 4

shrimp and coconut rice

4 tbsp. peanut oil
8 oz. Thai fragrant rice
1 tsp. cumin seeds
1 small cinnamon stick
4 lime leaves
14 oz. can coconut milk
½ cup water
1 tsp. salt
2 garlic cloves, crushed
1 in. piece of fresh ginger, peeled and grated
pinch of dried chili flakes
1 lb. raw tiger shrimp, peeled and deveined, (see page 33)
2 tbsp. Thai fish sauce
1 tbsp. lime juice
2 tbsp. chopped cilantro
1 oz. dry-roasted peanuts, chopped, to garnish

one Heat half the oil in a saucepan and stir-fry the rice until all the grains are glossy. Add the cumin seeds, cinnamon stick, lime leaves, coconut milk, water, and salt. Bring to a boil and simmer gently over low heat for 10 minutes. Remove from the heat, cover, and let rest for 10 minutes.

two Meanwhile, heat the remaining oil in a wok and stir-fry the garlic, ginger, and chili flakes for 30 seconds. Add the prawns and stir-fry for 3–4 minutes, until pink and just cooked through.

three Stir in the coconut rice with the fish sauce, lime juice, and cilantro and serve scattered with the peanuts.

Preparation time 2 minutes, plus chilling **Total time** 17 minutes **Serves** 4

melon with raspberries and monbazillac

2 baby Charentais or cantaloupe melons
4 oz. raspberries
1 cup chilled Monbazillac wine

The success of this recipe depends solely on the quality of the fresh fruit, so buy melons with a heavy scent, that feel firm but with a slight give.

one Cut the melons in half and scoop out the seeds. Spoon the raspberries into the hollows and top off with the dessert wine. Chill for at least 15 minutes before serving.

blueberry fool

8 oz. blueberries
strip of lemon rind
¼ cup sugar
juice of ½ lemon
1 cup heavy cream
Hazelnut Melts (see page 22) or
cookies, to serve

one Put the blueberries, lemon rind, and sugar in a pan and heat gently until the blueberries soften slightly. Plunge the base of the pan into iced water to cool.

two Set 4 tbsp. of the blueberries aside and transfer the rest to a food processor or blender, then add the lemon juice and process until a smooth purée is reached. Whip the cream until it starts to form peaks and fold in all the purée. Spoon into glasses, top with the reserved blueberries, and serve with hazelnut melts or cookies.

Preparation time 10 minutes, plus cooling Cooking time 3–4 minutes each side on grill,

6–8 minutes each side under the broiler Total time 18–26 minutes Serves 4

grilled fruits with palm sugar

2 tbsp. palm sugar
grated rind and juice of 1 lime
2 tbsp. water
½ tsp. cracked black peppercorns
1 lb. mixed prepared fruits
(such as pineapple slices, mango wedges,
and peaches)

To serve
cinnamon or vanilla ice cream
lime slices

one Warm the sugar, lime rind and juice, water, and peppercorns together in a small pan until the sugar has dissolved. Plunge the base of the pan into iced water to cool.

two Brush the cooled syrup over the prepared fruits and grill or broil until charred and tender. Serve with scoops of cinnamon or vanilla ice cream and slices of lime.

party
time

If you think preparing canapés and cocktails for larger groups is too time-consuming and not really worth it, then think again. All the dishes in this chapter are quick and easy to prepare and cook, so you can spend more time socializing with your friends than slaving over the proverbial hot stove.

Preparation time 5 minutes Cooking time 3 minutes Total time 8 minutes Serves 12

quail's eggs with spiced salt

24 quail's eggs
1 tsp. Szechuan peppercorns
2 tbsp. sea salt
½ tsp. Chinese five-spice powder

Szechuan peppercorns, also known as farchiew and anise pepper, are not really pepper, but the dried red berries of a type of ash tree. Nevertheless, they have a hot, peppery flavor, which is best brought out by dry-roasting in a cast-iron frying pan.

one Cook the eggs in a pan of gently simmering water for 3 minutes. Plunge them into cold water.

two Dry-fry the peppercorns until they are smoking. Cool and grind to a powder with the salt. Stir in the five-spice powder.

three Peel the eggs and serve with a bowl of the spiced salt, to dip.

Preparation time 10 minutes Cooking time 10 minutes Total time 20 minutes Makes 12

tuna and salsa verde toasts

1 large baguette
2 tbsp. extra virgin olive oil
8 oz. tuna steak
salt and pepper

Salsa verde
½ oz. parsley
2 tbsp. chopped mixed herbs (such as basil, chives, and mint)
1 garlic clove, crushed
½ oz. pitted green olives, chopped
2 anchovy fillets in oil, drained and chopped
½ tsp. Dijon mustard
1 tsp. white wine vinegar
¼ cup extra virgin olive oil

one Cut the baguette into thin slices, brush with some of the oil, and bake in a preheated 400°F oven for 8–10 minutes, until crisp and golden. Set aside to cool.

two Meanwhile, brush the tuna steak with a little oil, season to taste with salt and pepper, and sear in a hot griddle pan for 30 seconds on each side. Transfer to a plate and set aside to cool. (The tuna should be cooked on the outside, while still raw inside.)

three To make the salsa verde, put the parsley leaves, mixed herbs, garlic, olives, and anchovies into a food processor or blender and add the mustard, vinegar, and oil. Process to a purée and season to taste with salt and pepper.

four Dice the tuna and arrange on top of the toast with a little of the salsa verde.

Preparation time 12 minutes **Total time** 12 minutes **Makes** 24 canapés

chili crab tartlets

4 oz. fresh white crab meat
1 ripe tomato, peeled, seeded, and
finely chopped
1 small garlic clove, crushed
2 tbsp. chopped cilantro
¼–½ tsp. ground cayenne
4 tbsp. mayonnaise
a dash of lemon juice
24 cocktail tartlet cases
salt and pepper

one Carefully pick through the crab meat to remove any small pieces of cartilage that may remain.

two Add the tomato, garlic, cilantro, cayenne, and mayonnaise to the crab. Add a little lemon juice and season to taste with salt and pepper.

three Fill the cocktail tartlet cases with the crab mixture and serve.

open sushi

4 oz. sushi rice
1½ tbsp. rice wine vinegar
1 tbsp. sugar
1 tsp. salt
2 large sheets nori seaweed
2 oz. salmon fillet
about 2 tbsp. wasabi
12 cooked peeled shrimp
a few salmon eggs
pickled ginger (optional)
soy sauce, for dipping

Wasabi is a fiercely hot, green Japanese horseradish. It is available as a paste or a powder to which water is added.

one Cook the rice according to the instructions on the package. Drain well and immediately stir in the vinegar, sugar, and salt. Transfer to a bowl set in iced water and allow to cool for 10 minutes.

two Meanwhile, cut the nori sheets in half and then cut each half into six rectangles, to make 24 in total. Cut the salmon into small dice.

three Dot wasabi in the middle of each piece of nori, mound a spoonful of rice over this, and top half with the salmon and half with the prawns and salmon eggs. Add a sliver of ginger, if desired, and pull the edges of the nori up at each side.

four Arrange on a large platter and pass the sushi around with a bowl of soy sauce for dipping.

corn cakes with chili jam

1 quantity Chili Jam (see page 74)
4 lime leaves, very thinly shredded
½ cup plus 2 tbsp. self-rising flour
1 egg
1 tbsp. Thai fish sauce
1 tbsp. lime juice
5 oz. corn kernels
24 endive spears, about 2 heads
vegetable oil, for deep-frying
a few basil, mint, and cilantro sprigs

one First make the chili jam. Meanwhile, place the lime leaves, flour, egg, fish sauce, lime juice, and half the corn in a food processor or blender and process until fairly smooth.

two Transfer the mixture to a bowl and stir in the remaining corn. Heat 2 inches of oil in a wok and deep-fry teaspoons of the batter, in batches, for 1–2 minutes, or until golden. Drain on paper towels and keep warm while you are cooking the remainder.

three Place a corn cake in each chicory spear, top with chili jam and some fresh herbs and serve immediately.

90. party time

Preparation time 20 minutes, including marinating and cooling Cooking time 8 minutes

Total time 28 minutes Makes 20 canapés

tandoori chicken poppadums

2 skinless chicken breast fillets
1 small garlic clove, crushed
1 in. piece of fresh ginger,
peeled and grated
¼ cup yogurt
1 tsp. honey
1 tsp. tandoori spice powder
1 tsp. salt
½ quantity Coconut Pesto (see page 70)
20 mini poppadums

To serve
mango chutney
cilantro sprigs

Mini poppadums can be found in most large supermarkets. If they are unavailable, use large poppadums and carefully break them into bite-sized pieces.

one Score the chicken fillets several times with a sharp knife and place in a shallow bowl. Add the garlic, ginger, yogurt, honey, tandoori spice powder, and salt. Toss well and set aside to marinate for 10 minutes.

two Broil or grill the marinated chicken for 3–4 minutes each side and then cool for about 5 minutes.

three Meanwhile, make the coconut pesto. Slice the chicken and serve on the poppadums with a spoonful each of the pesto and mango chutney and a sprig of cilantro.

Preparation time 17 minutes Cooking time 2–4 minutes per batch

Total time 29 minutes Makes 12 parcels

crackling fish pockets

1 garlic clove, crushed
½ in. piece of fresh ginger, peeled and grated
2 tbsp. finely chopped mint
1 tbsp. sweet chili sauce
8 oz. skinless salmon fillets
12 small sheets rice flour pancakes
sunflower oil, for frying
salt and pepper

Dipping sauce
2 tbsp. light soy sauce
2 tbsp. mirin
4 tbsp. water
2 tbsp. palm sugar
½ tsp. dried chili flakes

Rice flour pancakes are wrapped around small fillets of spiced salmon and fried until crisp and golden.

one Place all the sauce ingredients in a small pan and heat gently to dissolve the sugar. Remove from the heat and set aside to cool.

two Meanwhile, mix together the garlic, ginger, mint, and chili sauce. Cut the salmon into 12 equal-sized pieces and coat with the spice paste.

three Soak the rice flour pancakes according to the package instructions. Place a piece of salmon fillet on each one, dampen the edges, and fold the pancake over and around the fish.

four Heat the oil and pan-fry the pockets, in batches, for 1–2 minutes on each side, or until golden and crisp. Let rest for a few minutes then serve with the dipping sauce.

smoked trout
and avocado blinis

½ avocado, peeled, pitted, and finely diced
1 scallion, thinly sliced
1 small garlic clove, crushed
1 tbsp. chopped dill
1 tsp. lime juice
2 tbsp. crème fraîche
6 oz. smoked trout fillets
24 cocktail blinis
salt and pepper
dill sprigs, to garnish

one Mix together the avocado, scallion, garlic, dill, lime juice, and crème fraîche and season to taste with salt and pepper.

two Flake the trout fillets into bite-sized pieces. Toast the blinis according to the package instructions and top each one with some trout and avocado cream. Garnish with dill sprigs and serve.

Preparation time 8 minutes Cooking time 3 minutes Total time 11 minutes Makes 12

sweet wonton millefeuille

1 tbsp. unsalted butter
2 tbsp. sugar
½ tsp. ground cinnamon
9 wonton wrappers
4 oz. mascarpone cheese
1–2 tbsp. powdered sugar, plus extra,
for dusting
1 tsp. lemon juice
4 oz. strawberries, hulled and sliced

one Melt the butter and mix the sugar and cinnamon together. Cut the wonton wrappers into quarters, brush with the butter, and coat with a layer of the spiced sugar.

two Place on a baking sheet and bake in a preheated 400°F oven for 2–3 minutes, or until crisp and golden. Cool on a wire rack.

three Beat the mascarpone with the powdered sugar and lemon juice and spread a little over 12 of the crisp wontons. Top with half of the strawberry slices. Repeat the process with the remaining mascarpone and strawberries for the second layer. Place the remaining wontons on top and dust with a little extra powdered sugar. Serve with glasses of champagne, if desired.

Preparation time 5 minutes Total time 5 minutes Serves 6

champagne with pomegranate syrup

1 small pomegranate
6 tsp. pomegranate syrup or grenadine
1 bottle chilled champagne

one Halve the pomegranate and scoop the seeds into a sieve. Using a wooden spoon crush the seeds to extract about 6 tbsp. of juice.

two Put a teaspoonful of pomegranate syrup or grenadine into the bottom of each of 6 glasses, top off with champagne, stir to dissolve the syrup, and add a little of the pomegranate juice. Serve immediately.

Preparation time 6 minutes Total time 6 minutes Serves 6

iced lemon and mint vodka

4 tbsp. lemon juice
8 tbsp. lemon cordial
4 fl oz. vodka, chilled
ice cubes
a few mint sprigs
tonic water

one Pour the lemon juice, cordial, and vodka into a cocktail shaker and shake well.

two Pour into 6 tall glasses half-filled with ice cubes. Add a few mint sprigs and top off with tonic water. Serve immediately.

peach and elderflower bellini

2 ripe peaches
4 tbsp. elderflower cordial
1 bottle chilled champagne
a few elderflowers, to garnish (optional)

one Plunge the peaches into boiling water for 1–2 minutes. Refresh under cold water and peel off the skins. Halve, pit, and coarsely chop the flesh.

two Put the peaches and elderflower cordial in a food processor and process to a fairly smooth purée. Divide the purée between 6 glasses. Top off with champagne and serve garnished with elderflowers, if desired.

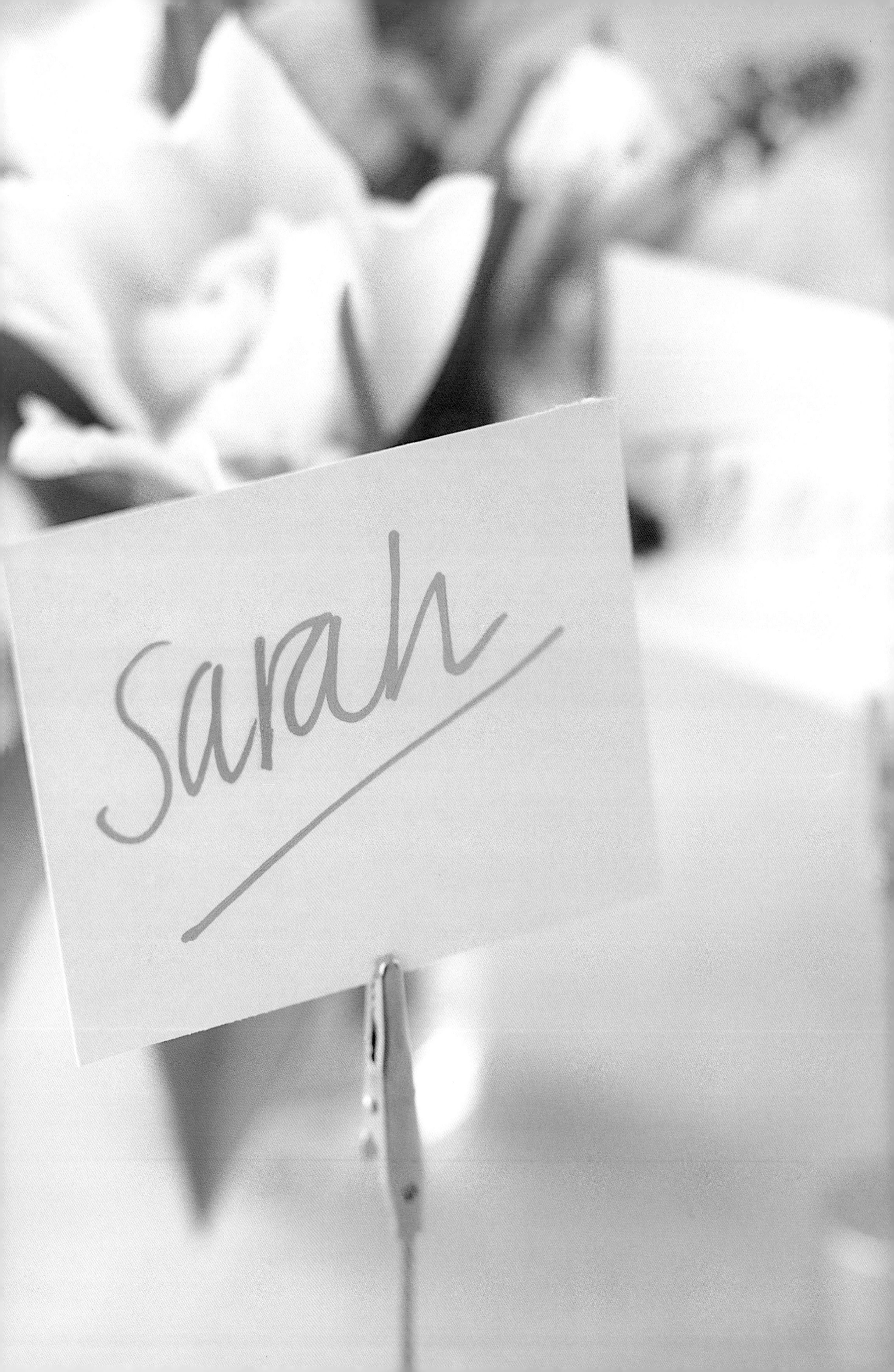
Sarah

posh nosh

Just because you are entertaining for a formal occasion, there is no need to spend days preparing the food. Nor do you need to worry about the flavor of the dishes being compromised by the length of time taken to make them. All of the following recipes are inspiring and delicious, so you can show off your skills without spending your whole day in preparation.

Preparation time 10 minutes Cooking time 2 minutes Total time 12 minutes Serves 4

steamed oysters with asian flavors

12 oysters, shucked
2 scallions, white parts only, thinly sliced
¾ in. piece of fresh
ginger, peeled and grated
1 small garlic clove, thinly sliced
1 small red chili, seeded and sliced
¼ cup sake
2 tbsp. rice vinegar
2 tsp. dark soy sauce
cilantro leaves, to garnish

Shucking is the name given to opening oysters. It is best done by the fishmonger, but ask him to reserve any juices.

one Remove the top shell from the shucked oysters and strain the juices through a fine sieve into a small pan. Carefully wipe out any grit that may still remain in the shells.

two Add the scallions, ginger, garlic, chili, sake, vinegar, and soy sauce to the oyster juices. Warm through gently.

three Arrange the oysters in a large bamboo steamer, cover and steam for 2 minutes. Transfer to plates, spoon over the sauce, and serve garnished with cilantro leaves.

Preparation time 15 minutes, including cooling Cooking time 2 minutes per batch

Total time 23–25 minutes Serves 4

salt and pepper squid

1½ lb prepared squid
4 tbsp. all-purpose flour
1 tbsp. sea salt
2 tsp. white pepper
pinch of Chinese five-spice powder
vegetable oil, for deep-frying
lime wedges, to serve

Chili dipping sauce
½ small onion, finely chopped
1 garlic clove, finely chopped
1 tbsp. kecap manis
1 tbsp. dark soy sauce
1 tsp. brown sugar
1 tsp. sesame oil

Ready-prepared squid is available from the fish department of many large supermarkets. Alternatively, ask the fishmonger to clean the squid for you.

one First, make the chili dipping sauce. Mix all the ingredients in a small pan and simmer for 8–10 minutes, or until reduced and thickened. Plunge the pan into cold water to cool the sauce.

two Slice the prepared squid into rings. Sift the flour, salt, pepper, and five-spice powder together.

three Dip the squid pieces into the spiced flour and deep-fry in hot oil, in batches if necessary, for 1–2 minutes, or until crisp. Drain on paper towels and keep warm while you cook the remainder. Serve with the dipping sauce.

Preparation time 15 minutes, including cooling Total time 15 minutes Serves 4 as a starter

thai shrimp and papaya salad

1 small green papaya, peeled, seeded, and thinly shredded
1 red onion, thinly sliced
1 garlic clove, sliced
2–4 small red chilies, seeded, and thinly sliced
¾ in. piece of fresh ginger, peeled, and cut into thin strips
small bunch of cilantro, chopped
8 oz. cooked peeled tiger shrimp, deveined (see page 33)

Dressing
3 tbsp. palm sugar
2½ tbsp. rice vinegar
2½ tbsp. lime juice
½ tsp. salt

one First, make the dressing. Put all the ingredients in a small pan and warm through just long enough to dissolve the sugar. Plunge the pan into iced water and set aside to cool.

two Mix together the papaya, onion, garlic, chilies, ginger, and cilantro in a large bowl. Stir in the shrimp and the cooled dressing. Mix together and serve.

Preparation time 10 minutes Cooking time 10 minutes Total time 20 minutes Serves 4

scallops with ginger and asparagus

12 fresh scallops
2 scallions, thinly sliced
finely grated rind of 1 lime
1 tbsp. ginger cordial
2 tbsp. extra virgin olive oil, plus
extra for drizzling
8 oz. thin asparagus spears
juice of ½ lime
a few mixed salad greens
a few chervil sprigs
salt and pepper

one Wash the scallops and pat dry. Cut each one in half and place in a bowl.

two Mix together the scallions, lime rind, ginger cordial, and half the oil and season to taste with salt and pepper. Pour over the scallops and set aside to marinate for 15 minutes.

three Meanwhile, steam the asparagus spears for 5–8 minutes, or until tender. Toss with the remaining oil and the lime juice. Season to taste with salt and pepper and keep warm.

four Heat a large nonstick frying pan until hot, add the scallops and sauté for 1 minute on each side, or until golden and just cooked through. Add the marinade juices.

five Arrange the asparagus spears, salad greens, and chervil on plates. Top with the scallops and any pan juices and serve.

Preparation time 15 minutes Cooking time 8 minutes, plus resting Total time 28 minutes Serves 4

blackened cod with orange and tomato salsa

1 large orange
1 garlic clove, crushed
2 large tomatoes, peeled, seeded, and diced
2 tbsp. chopped basil
2 oz. pitted black olives, chopped
5 tbsp. extra virgin olive oil
4 cod fillets, about 6 oz. each
1 tbsp. jerk seasoning
salt and pepper
basil leaves, to garnish
a green salad, to serve (optional)

Choose thick fillets of cod from the head end of the fish.

one Peel and segment the orange, holding it over a bowl to catch the juices. Halve the segments. Mix them with the garlic, tomatoes, basil, olives, and 4 tbsp. of the oil, season to taste with salt and pepper and set aside to infuse.

two Wash and pat dry the fish and pull out any small bones with a pair of tweezers. Brush with the remaining oil and coat well with the jerk seasoning.

three Heat a large heavy-bottomed pan and pan-fry the cod fillets, skin-side down, for 5 minutes. Turn them over and cook for another 3 minutes. Transfer to a low oven, 300°F, to rest for about 5 minutes.

four Garnish the fish with basil and serve with the salsa and a green salad, if desired.

Preparation time 5 minutes Cooking time 20 minutes Total time 25 minutes Serves 4

poached fish in miso

8 oz. Thai fragrant rice
1¾ cup fish stock
1 tbsp. dark soy sauce
1 tbsp. mirin
½ tbsp. brown rice vinegar
½ tbsp. barley miso
1 star anise
1 tbsp. sunflower oil
4 salmon fillets, about 5 oz. each
2 tsp. black sesame seeds
salt and pepper
steamed Chinese cabbage, to serve

one Cook the rice according to the package instructions and keep warm.

two Put the stock, soy sauce, mirin, vinegar, miso, and star anise into a saucepan and bring to a boil, then cover and simmer for 5 minutes.

three Heat the oil in a frying pan and sear the salmon fillets for 1 minute on each side. Transfer to the stock, then remove the pan from the heat, but allow the salmon fillets to poach in the hot stock for 1 minute.

four Stir the sesame seeds into the cooked rice and spoon into soup plates. Top with the poached salmon and pour in the stock. Serve immediately with steamed Chinese cabbage.

Preparation time 10 minutes Cooking time 3–5 minutes Total time 15 minutes Serves 4

summer pasta of zucchini and dill

8 tbsp. extra virgin olive oil
4 garlic cloves, sliced
4 zucchini
4 zucchini flowers (optional)
4 tbsp. chopped dill
1 lb fresh tagliatelle
dash of lemon juice
salt and pepper
freshly grated Parmesan cheese, to serve

Use fresh pasta only if you know that the quality is good or if it is homemade. Alternatively, use a dried egg pasta. If using dried pasta, start cooking it before preparing the remaining ingredients.

one Heat the oil, add the garlic and sauté for 1–2 minutes, until lightly golden. Remove the pan from the heat and set aside. Coarsely grate the zucchini and thinly slice the flowers, if using.

two Meanwhile, cook the tagliatelle in a large pan of lightly salted boiling water for 3 minutes, or until tender but still firm to the bite. Drain well and return to the pan.

three Immediately stir in the garlic and oil, zucchini, zucchini flowers, and dill. Season to taste with lemon juice, salt, and pepper. Sprinkle over plenty of Parmesan cheese and serve immediately.

Preparation time 5 minutes Cooking time 20 minutes Total time 25 minutes Serves 4

duck breast with glazed quince

4 duck breast fillets, about 8 oz. each
1 tsp. salt
1 medium quince, peeled, cored, and cut into wedges
2 tbsp. quince paste or honey
½ cup red wine
¾ cup plus 2 tbsp. chicken stock
Creamy Mashed Potatoes, to serve (see right)

To make creamy mashed potatoes, cook and mash the potatoes in the normal way, but beat in 4–6 tbsp. heavy cream with the butter, salt, and pepper.

one Score the duck skin with several slashes and rub all over with salt. Pan-fry, skin-side down, in a hot frying pan for 6 minutes. Turn and cook for another 3 minutes. Remove from the pan and keep warm.

two Discard all but 1 tbsp. of the duck fat. Add the quince and brown quickly on all sides. Stir in the quince paste or honey and wine and bring to a boil. Simmer gently until the quince is tender.

three Remove the quince with a slotted spoon and keep warm. Add the stock to the pan and boil until slightly reduced and thickened. Slice the duck and serve with the glazed quince, the pan juices, and creamy mashed potatoes.

Preparation time 8 minutes Cooking time 19 minutes Total time 27 minutes Serves 4

cilantro chicken pockets with roasted vine tomatoes

4 bunches cherry tomatoes on the vine
2 tbsp. extra virgin olive oil
4 skinless chicken breast fillets
1 garlic clove, crushed
2 tbsp. chopped cilantro
2 tbsp. softened unsalted butter
pinch of ground cayenne pepper
8 slices prosciutto
salt and pepper

one Place the tomatoes, still attached to the vine, in a large roasting tin, drizzle over half the oil, and season with salt and pepper. Set aside. Make a horizontal slit into the thickest side of each chicken breast.

two Beat the garlic and cilantro into the butter with the cayenne pepper and some salt. Divide the flavored butter into four, pat flat, and slip a piece into each chicken breast.

three Wrap 2 slices of prosciutto around each breast and secure with toothpicks. Heat the remaining oil in a frying pan and brown the chicken pockets for 2 minutes on each side.

four Add the chicken to the tomatoes and roast in a preheated 400°F oven for 10 minutes, or until the chicken is cooked through. Remove the chicken, wrap loosely in foil, and let rest. Roast the tomatoes for another 5 minutes.

five Remove the toothpicks and serve the chicken with the tomatoes and the pan juices.

Preparation time 5 minutes Cooking time 20 minutes, plus 5 minutes resting

Total time 20 minutes Serves 4

lamb fillet with beets and mint salad

4 oz. Puy lentils
4 oz. small green beans
4 tbsp. extra virgin olive oil
2 lamb fillets (best end), about 10 oz. each
4 tbsp. red wine
1 tbsp. red wine vinegar
12 oz. cooked beets in natural juices, drained and diced
a small bunch mint, coarsely chopped
salt and pepper

The cut of meat you need for this dish is the best end of neck fillet or lamb loins. It is the eye fillet of the cutlets that make up a rack, and is quite an expensive cut. You can ask to keep the ribs to cook as grilled spare ribs.

one Put the lentils in a pan, cover with cold water, and simmer for 20 minutes. Drain well and place in a bowl.

two Meanwhile, blanch the beans in lightly salted boiling water for 3 minutes. Drain and pat dry.

three Heat 1 tbsp. of the oil in a frying pan and pan-fry the lamb fillets for 7 minutes for rare lamb. Transfer to a low oven, 300°F, to rest for 5 minutes, reserving the juices in the pan.

four Add the wine to the pan and boil until only about 1 tbsp. remains. Remove from the heat and whisk in the vinegar and the remaining oil and season to taste with salt and pepper.

five Combine the lentils, beans, beets, and mint leaves in a bowl, add the dressing and toss to coat evenly. Serve with the lamb.

Preparation time 10 minutes Cooking time 4 minutes Total time 14 minutes Serves 4

fillet steak with blue cheese and walnut sauce

1 tablespoon butter
4 fillet steaks
new potatoes, to serve

Blue cheese and walnut sauce
1 garlic clove, crushed
1 oz. parsley leaves, coarsely chopped
½ oz. mint leaves, coarsely chopped
1 tbsp. coarsely chopped walnuts
6 tablespoons extra virgin olive oil
2 tbsp. walnut oil
2 oz. Roquefort cheese, crumbled
½ oz. Parmesan cheese, grated
salt and pepper

Store the rest of the sauce, topped with a layer of oil, in a screw-top jar for up to 5 days. Serve tossed with fresh pasta noodles.

one First, make the sauce. Put the garlic, parsley, mint, walnuts, and both oils in a food processor and process until fairly smooth.

two Add the Roquefort and Parmesan and then process again. Season to taste with salt and pepper.

three Melt the butter in a heavy-bottomed frying pan. Season the steaks with salt and pepper and pan-fry for 2 minutes on each side for rare, or a little longer for medium rare. Transfer to plates, top with the cheese sauce, and serve with new potatoes.

Preparation time 10 minutes Cooking time 5 minutes, plus cooling

Total time 25 minutes Serves 4

poached apricots with rosewater and pistachio

½ cup sugar
1 cup water
2 strips lemon rind
2 cardamom pods
1 vanilla pod
12 apricots, halved and pitted
1 tbsp. lemon juice
1 tbsp. rosewater
1 oz. shelled pistachio nuts, finely chopped
vanilla ice cream or yogurt, to
serve (optional)

one Put a large bowl into the freezer to chill. Put the sugar and water into a wide saucepan and heat gently to dissolve the sugar. Meanwhile, cut the lemon rind into thin strips, crush the cardamom pods, and split the vanilla pod in half. Add the lemon rind, cardamom, and vanilla pod to the pan.

two Add the apricots and simmer gently for about 5 minutes, or until softened. Remove from the heat, add the lemon juice and rosewater, and transfer to the chilled bowl. Leave to cool until required.

three Spoon the apricots and a little of the syrup into serving bowls, scatter over the nuts, and serve with ice cream or yogurt, if desired.

Preparation time 12 minutes Cooking time 15 minutes Total time 27 minutes Serves 6

chocolate rum soufflés

4 oz. dark chocolate
2 tbsp. butter, plus extra for greasing
4 eggs, separated
6 tbsp. sugar
2 tbsp. rum
whipped cream, to serve

one Melt the chocolate and butter in a small saucepan over a low heat. Meanwhile, beat together the egg yolks and sugar until creamy, then stir in the rum and melted chocolate mixture.

two Whisk the egg whites until stiff and fold into the chocolate mixture until evenly incorporated. Spoon into 6 greased ramekins and bake in a preheated 400°F oven for 15 minutes, or until puffed. Serve immediately with whipped cream.

tiramisu trifles

8 amaretti biscuits
2 tbsp. Marsala wine
2 tbsp. cold espresso coffee
3 oz. raspberries
2 oz. dark chocolate, grated
4 oz. mascarpone cheese
½ cup crème fraîche
1 oz. powdered sugar
2 egg whites

one Lightly crumble the amaretti biscuits into 4 glasses. Mix the Marsala and coffee together and pour half over the biscuits. Add the raspberries and sprinkle half the grated chocolate over the top.

two Beat the mascarpone, crème fraîche, and the remaining Marsala mixture with the powdered sugar until smooth. Whisk the egg whites until stiff, then fold into the Marsala cream, and spoon into the glasses.

three Sprinkle over the remaining chocolate and chill until served.

honeyed peaches with ginger cream

4 ripe peaches
2 tbsp. honey
seeds from 1 vanilla pod
juice of ½ lime
½ cup heavy cream
1 tbsp. stem ginger syrup, from the jar
1 small piece stem ginger, diced

one Cut the peaches in half, remove the pits, and arrange the halves, cut-side up, in an ovenproof dish.

two Combine the honey, vanilla seeds, and lime juice and spoon over the peaches. Bake in a preheated 425°F oven for 25 minutes.

three Whip the cream with the ginger syrup until it holds its shape. Fold the stem ginger into the cream and serve with the baked peaches.

pantry suppers

Don't be concerned about the occasional last minute arrival; your pantry will most probably contain enough raw materials to put together a delicious impromptu feast. Beans, grains, and pastas are all staples that keep well and can be transformed into some of our favorite dishes. Remember, too, if one of the following recipes calls for an ingredient you don't have, then ad lib and substitute an equivalent that you do have.

Preparation time 4 minutes Cooking time 4 minutes Total time 8 minutes Serves 4 as a starter

fava bean hummus

8 oz. fava beans
1 garlic clove, crushed
2 tbsp. chopped mint
1 tbsp. lemon juice
4 tbsp. extra virgin olive oil
1 oz. Parmesan cheese, grated
salt and pepper

To serve
vegetable crudités
bread sticks

This bean hummus is particularly versatile, as it can served as a dip with a selection of crudités, as a sandwich filling, or a sauce for pasta.

one Cook the beans in a pan of lightly salted boiling water for 3–4 minutes, until tender. Drain and refresh in cold water, then pat dry with paper towels.

two Place the beans, garlic, mint, lemon juice, and oil in a food processor or blender and process to form a smooth paste.

three Transfer to a bowl, add the cheese, and season to taste with salt and pepper. Serve with a selection of vegetable crudités and bread sticks for dipping.

Preparation time 7 minutes Cooking time 6 minutes Total time 13 minutes Serves 2

artichoke and blue cheese panini

13 oz. can artichoke hearts, drained and rinsed
4 oz. cambozola or dolcelatte cheese
1 small ripe pear
2 focaccia rolls
a few watercress sprigs
salt and pepper

one Pat the artichokes dry and cut into thin slices. Thinly slice the cheese. Peel, core, and thinly slice the pear.

two Halve the focaccia and toast the cut sides in a hot griddle pan or under a hot broiler. Fill with the artichokes, cheese, pear slices, and watercress. Season to taste with salt and pepper and sandwich together.

three Lower the heat and griddle the whole rolls for 2 minutes on each side, or until toasted and the cheese starts to melt.

tomato and bacon sauce for pasta

2 garlic cloves, crushed
2 13 oz. cans chopped tomatoes
4 tbsp. extra virgin olive oil
1 teaspoon dried oregano
1 teaspoon sugar
8 slices bacon, finely chopped
3 oz. mascarpone cheese
or 6 tbsp. crème fraîche
salt and pepper
pasta, to serve

This is a good basic sauce for pasta and can be made without the bacon for vegetarians. I often make up several batches, minus the mascarpone or crème fraîche, and freeze it for future use.

one Put the garlic, tomatoes, oil, oregano, and sugar in a saucepan. Season to taste with salt and pepper and bring to a boil, cover and simmer for 10 minutes.

two Add the bacon and simmer, uncovered, for another 5 minutes.

three Stir in the mascarpone or crème fraîche, heat through, then taste and adjust the seasoning if necessary. Serve with freshly cooked pasta.

Preparation time 8 minutes Cooking time 22 minutes Total time 30 minutes Serves 3–4

chili bean soup

2 tbsp. olive oil
1 onion, chopped
1 garlic clove, crushed
1 teaspoon hot chili powder
1 teaspoon ground coriander
½ teaspoon ground cumin
13 oz. can red kidney beans, drained
13 oz. can chopped tomatoes
2 cups vegetable stock
12 tortilla chips
2 oz. cheddar cheese, grated
salt and pepper
sour cream, to serve

one Heat the oil in a saucepan and sauté the onion, garlic, chili powder, coriander, and cumin, stirring frequently, for 5 minutes, or until the onion has softened. Add the beans, tomatoes, and stock and season to taste with salt and pepper.

two Bring to a boil, cover and simmer for 15 minutes. Transfer to a food processor or blender and process until fairly smooth. Pour into heat-proof bowls.

three Place tortilla chips on top of the soup, scatter over the grated cheese, and broil for 1–2 minutes or until the cheese has melted. Serve immediately with sour cream.

Preparation time 10 minutes Cooking time 11 minutes Total time 21 minutes Serves 4

smoked tuna and bean salad

8 oz. baby new potatoes
4 oz. small green beans
2 4 oz. cans smoked tuna in olive oil, drained
13 oz. can cranberry or navy beans, drained
4 ripe plum tomatoes, coarsely chopped
2 oz. Niçoise olives
2 tbsp. capers in brine, drained and rinsed

Dressing
2 sun-dried tomatoes in oil, drained and coarsely chopped
1 small garlic clove, crushed
½ teaspoon dried oregano
1 tbsp. white wine vinegar
pinch of sugar
6 tbsp. extra virgin olive oil
salt and pepper

Smoked tuna is available in cans from most large supermarkets. The more traditional canned tuna can be used, but buy tuna packed in olive oil.

one Cook the potatoes in a pan of lightly salted boiling water for 8 minutes. Add the green beans and cook for another 3 minutes, or until both the potatoes and beans are tender. Drain and refresh in cold water, drain again, then pat dry and place in a large bowl.

two Meanwhile, flake the tuna. Add the tuna, beans, tomatoes, olives, and capers to the potatoes.

three Make the dressing. Put the sun-dried tomatoes, garlic, oregano, vinegar, sugar, and oil in a food processor or blender and process to a purée. Season to taste with salt and pepper. Pour the dressing over the salad, toss well, and serve.

Preparation time 5 minutes Cooking time 20 minutes Total time 25 minutes Serves 4

individual macaroni cheeses

8 oz. macaroni
4 slices bacon, diced
1 garlic clove, crushed
½ cup light cream
½ cup milk
pinch of freshly grated nutmeg
6 oz. hard cheese, such as cheddar or
Gruyère, grated
4 tbsp. chopped basil
salt and pepper

one Cook the macaroni in a pan of lightly salted boiling water for 10–12 minutes, until tender but still firm to the bite. Drain and place in a large bowl.

two Meanwhile, pan-fry the bacon in a small frying pan until browned but not crisp. Add the garlic, sauté for 1 minute, and then add the cream and milk and season with a little nutmeg. Bring just to the boiling point.

three Stir in 4 oz. of the cheese and all the basil, remove from the heat and stir until the cheese melts. Season to taste with salt and pepper and stir into the macaroni.

four Spoon into individual gratin dishes, top with the remaining cheese and bake in a preheated 450°F oven for 10 minutes, or until golden.

Preparation time 10 minutes Cooking time 18 minutes Total time 28 minutes Serves 4

spicy tuna fish cakes

8 oz. baking potatoes, peeled and diced
2 7 oz. cans tuna in olive oil, drained
2 oz. cheddar cheese, grated
4 scallions, finely chopped
1 small garlic clove, crushed
2 teaspoons dried thyme
1 small egg, beaten
½ teaspoon cayenne pepper
4 tbsp. seasoned flour
salt and pepper
vegetable oil, for frying

To serve
mixed green salad
mayonnaise

one Cook the potatoes in a pan of lightly salted boiling water for 10 minutes, or until tender. Drain well, mash, and cool slightly.

two Meanwhile, flake the tuna. Beat the tuna, cheese, scallions, garlic, thyme, and egg into the mashed potatoes. Season to taste with cayenne, salt, and pepper.

three Divide the mixture into 4 and shape into thick patties. Dust with seasoned flour and fry in a shallow layer of vegetable oil for 5 minutes on each side, or until crisp and golden. Serve hot with a mixed green salad and mayonnaise.

asian-style risotto

4 cups hot vegetable stock
1 tbsp. dark soy sauce
2 tbsp. mirin
3 tbsp. sunflower oil
1 tbsp. sesame oil
1 bunch scallions, thickly sliced
2 garlic cloves, chopped
1 in. piece of fresh ginger,
peeled and grated
12 oz. arborio rice
6 lime leaves
8 oz. shiitake mushrooms
½ oz. cilantro, chopped
cilantro sprigs, to garnish

one Put the stock, soy sauce, and mirin into a pan and bring to a very gentle simmer.

two Meanwhile, heat 2 tbsp. of the sunflower oil and the sesame oil and sauté the onions, garlic, and ginger over high heat for 1 minute. Add the rice and lime leaves, stir until the grains are glossy, then add ½ cup of the stock. Stir until the liquid has been absorbed.

three Continue to add the stock, a little at a time, stirring frequently, until almost all the liquid is absorbed.

four Meanwhile, wipe the mushrooms, discard the stems, and thinly slice all but a few. Sauté all the mushrooms in the remaining oil, for 5 minutes or until golden.

five Add the cilantro to the risotto with the mushrooms and the remaining stock. Heat through and serve garnished with the whole mushrooms and a cilantro sprig.

mushroom and chickpea curry with aromatic rice

2 tbsp. butter
1 onion, chopped
2 garlic cloves, crushed
1 in. piece of fresh ginger, peeled and grated
8 oz. button mushrooms
2 tbsp. hot curry powder
1 teaspoon ground coriander
1 teaspoon ground cinnamon
12 oz. potatoes, diced
13 oz. can chickpeas, drained
2 oz. cashew nuts
½ cup yogurt
2 unripe bananas, cut into chunks
chopped cilantro (optional)
salt and pepper

Aromatic rice
12 oz. long grain rice
12 dried curry leaves
3 cardamom pods, crushed
1 cinnamon stick, crushed
1 teaspoon salt
3 cups water

one First cook the rice. Place the rice in a saucepan with the curry leaves, spices, and salt. Add the water, bring to a boil, cover, and cook over low heat for 10 minutes. Remove the pan from the heat, but leave the rice undisturbed for another 10 minutes.

two Meanwhile, melt the butter in a frying pan and sauté the onion, garlic, ginger, and mushrooms for 5 minutes.

three Add the curry powder, ground coriander, cinnamon, and potatoes, stir, and then add the chickpeas. Season to taste with salt and pepper and add just enough water to cover. Bring to a boil, cover, and simmer gently for 15 minutes.

four While the curry is cooking, toast and coarsely chop the cashew nuts. Stir them into the curry with the yogurt, bananas, and chopped cilantro, if using. Heat through without boiling and serve with the rice.

Preparation time 3 minutes **Cooking time** 10 minutes **Total time** 13 minutes **Serves** 4

mustard rarebit with caraway

1 tbsp. butter
4 scallions, thinly sliced
½ tsp. caraway seeds
8 oz. cheddar or red Leicester cheese, grated
¼ cup strong ale
2 tsp. wholegrain mustard
4 slices white bread
pepper

one Melt the butter in a small pan, add the scallions and caraway seeds, and sauté for 5 minutes, or until the onions have softened.

two Stir in the cheese with the beer and mustard, season with pepper to taste, and melt over very low heat.

three Meanwhile, toast the bread lightly on both sides and place on a foil-lined broiler pan. Pour over the cheese mixture and broil for 1 minute, until bubbling and golden.

leek and goat cheese frittata

1 tbsp. butter
2 leeks, sliced
1 garlic clove, crushed
1 tsp. chopped thyme
6 eggs
2 tbsp. chopped parsley
4 oz. goat cheese, sliced
1 oz. pitted black olives, halved
salt and pepper

one Melt the butter in a frying pan and sauté the leeks, garlic, and thyme for 10 minutes, or until the leeks have softened.

two Meanwhile, beat the eggs with the parsley and salt and pepper to taste.

three Swirl the egg mixture into the pan and cook for 3–4 minutes, or until almost set through. Top with the goat cheese and olives and cook under a hot broiler for another 2–3 minutes, or until bubbling, golden, and set.

sticky toffee puddings

4 tbsp. heavy cream, plus extra to serve
2 tbsp. butter, separated into quarters
4 tbsp. soft light brown sugar

Sponge
1 oz. walnuts, finely chopped
4 tbsp. softened butter
½ cup plus 1 tbsp. soft light brown sugar
2 eggs
¾ cup self-rising flour

Surprisingly quick to prepare and cook, these nutty sticky puddings are really yummy!

one Divide the cream, butter, and sugar evenly between 4 ramekins or timbales.

two To make the sponge, put the walnuts, butter, sugar, eggs, and flour in a food processor and process until smooth. Spoon the sponge mixture over the toffee mixture and smooth flat.

three Bake in a preheated 375°F oven for 20–25 minutes, or until puffed and lightly golden. Turn out and serve with the extra cream, lightly whipped.

index

index